770690

D1279555

Flexible
working hours

Heinz Allenspach

International Labour Office   Geneva

ISBN 92-2-101198-4

First published 1975

Printed by Maison d'Edition, 6001 Marcinelle (Belgium)

CONTENTS

INTRODUCTION

The system of flexible working hours is still very much of a novelty—so much so that its importance and potentialities are not always appreciated at their true worth and that the fundamental transformations which its introduction may entail often fail to be perceived. Yet there can be no doubt that flexible working time exercises an irreversible influence on the relationship between individuals and their jobs: the Director-General of the International Labour Office rightly referred to the system in his report to the Second European Regional Conference of the ILO as "the most radical innovation in the arrangement of working hours in recent years". [1] The fact is that the introduction of flexible working hours has the effect of throwing overboard the rules of punctual starting and finishing work that were established at a time when industrial undertakings were managed in an authoritarian way and with a view to optimum utilisation of the equipment. It presupposes the application of concerted methods of management designed to adapt work to the natural pace of the worker's daily life, so that instead of an external constraint imposed by the need to earn a living, work may become a means of self-fulfilment for the individual.

Moreover, by enabling individual workers to organise their working lives in a way better corresponding to their wishes, the system of flexible working hours affords them fuller opportunities of exercising their free will. Running thus counter to the increasing constraints of organisation and technique which are a notable feature of modern society, it is based on principles going far beyond those governing the usual employer-worker relations.

Furthermore, the flexible working hours system implies freely accepted co-operation within both formal and informal work groups: a corollary of

---

[1] ILO: *Human values in social policy: An ILO agenda for Europe*, Report of the Director-General of the ILO to the Second European Regional Conference (Geneva, 1974), p. 43.

the individual decisions to which the system gives rise is a voluntary sub-ordination to common needs. The system can be regarded in many cases as an attempt to reconcile as much as possible, at any rate in a limited field, the workers' own promptings with the organisational and technical require-ments of performance of a task during a given period.

In this study, which is based primarily on experiments made in Swiss enterprises, an attempt is made, first of all, to define the system of flexible working hours as applied in present-day circumstances and then to indicate its main practical features. A special chapter is devoted to the advantages and disadvantages of the system for workers, employers and the economy as a whole. The last chapter deals with special problems which introduction of the system raises with regard not only to the organisation of work and the communication of information to, and consultation with, the workers concerned, but also to the checks which the system requires.

THE CONCEPT AND THE SYSTEM

1

The system of flexible working hours stems from practical needs inherent in the operation of certain enterprises. Its introduction was not preceded by systematic research and the elaboration of carefully prepared models. Consequently, the principles which were in fact applied were described more or less pragmatically and in the light of the most obvious differences from earlier practice, with the result that various designations were applied to the same concept or, conversely, that the same designations covered various concepts. Only subsequently was an attempt made to achieve uniformity of concepts and designations. It has not yet been possible, however, to achieve general agreement on this question, so that the terminology employed continues to vary widely with the undertaking.

An attempt is made in these pages to attach exact definitions to concepts and their content, not so much in the interests of systematisation but for the purpose of better identifying, explaining and analysing the problems that arise.

For the purposes of this study, the starting point adopted consists in two fundamental and clearly distinguishable concepts, namely the length of hours of work on the one hand and the arrangement of working time on the other.

DIFFERENT KINDS OF HOURS OF WORK

In addition to the usual senses in which reference is made to normal hours of work, overtime and maximum hours of work, reference will be made in this study to hours of work in the following senses:

(*a*) actual hours of work, or the number of hours actually worked;

(*b*) prescribed hours of work, that is, the number of hours that must be worked by virtue of legislation or of an individual contract or of a collective agreement; and

(c) hours of work paid for, which generally exceed the number of hours actually worked where, for certain reasons, hours not worked (short absences, days of rest, holidays and absences due to sickness or accidents, etc.) must be treated as hours worked, and paid for as such.

These various definitions of hours of work may refer to the work day, the work week, or the wage payment period.

Actual hours of work also include, by definition, the amount of overtime worked. In many cases, however, they are limited to prescribed or normal hours of work so that, for technical reasons relating to pay calculations, overtime is treated separately instead of being included in actual hours of work.

As a rule, the number of hours of work paid for is greater than the number of actual hours of work to the extent that absences are paid in the same way as actual hours of work. Moreover, if overtime is included, the number of hours of work paid for may be greater than the number of prescribed or normal hours of work; but it may also be smaller than either the one or the other in the event of unremunerated absences.

When they are the number of hours provided for in an individual contract, the prescribed hours of work are often shorter than the normal hours as laid down in legislation. When the prescribed hours of work are shorter than the normal hours as laid down by law, the number of hours worked in excess of the prescribed number up to the limit of the normal number is often treated as contractual overtime, which is generally subject, so far as its timing and increased payment are concerned, to rules other than those relating to additional hours worked over and above the normal statutory hours.

FIXED AND FLEXIBLE HOURS

There are important differences between fixed and flexible hours of work. Hours of work are said to be fixed when the prescribed number of hours remains unchanged for some time. The prescribed number of hours of work can be fixed at, for example, eight a day. It is, however, also possible to fix the number by the week or by the month by distributing the hours unevenly over the working days. In that case, the question that arises is whether it is the employer or the worker who decides the hours to be worked on this or that day. If the employer requires overtime to be worked, his decision can be regarded as involving a change of the prescribed daily hours of work, especially if, during the accounting period or in the course of a certain length of time, the overtime is offset by corresponding holidays. In general, however, this practice is not described as constituting "flexible hours of work"; that expression is used only when the worker himself decides the number of hours which he proposes to work on this or that day, subject to subsequent make-up work time during the accounting period.

Part-time work is often wrongly assimilated to flexible hours of work. In fact, there can be part-time work only when the number of hours worked per day or per week or during the accounting period is smaller than the usual number and, consequently, represents only a part of the hours of work prescribed for the majority of the workers or for the permanent staff of the undertaking. This part can consist of part-time work carried out according to an imposed daily or weekly number of hours (for example, four hours a day on five days or eight hours a day on three specified working days); part-time work can also be carried out in accordance with a varied schedule, especially when the workers themselves decide how many hours they shall work on particular working days within the limits of the reduced number of hours of work that has been agreed for part-time employment.

The system of flexible hours nearly always involves a daily number of hours of work which varies in accordance with the worker's wishes, on the understanding that the hours are made up for in the course of an accounting period of one month.

RIGIDITY OR FLEXIBILITY IN THE ARRANGEMENT OF WORKING TIME

A working schedule consists in particular in a daily or weekly distribution of hours to be worked under the terms of a contract or collective agreement. Thus if, for example, the daily number of hours of work is eight, the schedule could be from 8 a.m. to noon and from 1 p.m. to 5 p.m.

As a rule, the schedule is not expressly specified in labour legislation. It is nevertheless influenced and limited by provisions relating to such matters as the daily period of rest, breaks, night work and maximum daily hours.

Working time can be scheduled in advance. This amounts to prescribing a timetable of hours of work for a certain length of time. Nevertheless, a fixed schedule of hours does not necessarily imply an even distribution of hours over the days of the week. The distribution can well be uneven, provided that the hours to be worked each day are specified. In the services sector hours of work are frequently fixed under a schedule that varies with the day of the week.

Fixed hours of work can apply to an undertaking as a whole. There are, however, also many cases in which hours of work vary with the department or the category of workers. Hours of work are then said to be staggered. It also frequently happens that there are individual hours of work, that is, hours suited to the needs and wishes of each worker. For practical reasons this is generally feasible only in small and medium-sized undertakings. However, since these hours of work are also rigidly fixed for a certain period, they can be said to be scheduled.

Where working time is not governed by a strict schedule, use is made of the term "flexible working hours", which means that the hours to be worked are determined from day to day.

The distinction having been made between rigid and flexible arrangement of working time, that is, between hours to be worked in accordance with a predetermined schedule and working hours determined from day to day, there remains the question of who is competent to act in the matter.

The scheduling of hours of work was, for a very long time, one of the employer's prerogatives: it was considered that one of the workers' duties was to do their work at times specified by the employer. Originally, the latter could fix hours of work as he pleased for each day of the week; this he often did when the worker lived under his roof. Subsequently, the employer was required by labour legislation to determine in advance how many hours should be worked, to schedule them accordingly and to give reasonably early notice of them to the workers.

In recent years, this right of the employer has in many cases undergone restrictions in the sense that the schedule of hours of work has been agreed with the worker personally, sometimes in the contract of employment, or in the sense that any modification of hours is subject to consultations with the workers or their representatives, or even to their consent. This obligation to consult the workers, and if necessary to obtain their agreement, may be laid down by law, or it may simply result from the state of the employment market. In fact, the employer's discretionary power has increasingly been superseded by agreements concerning the arrangement of working time, though these agreements have generally been concerned with the establishment of a fixed schedule.

Some employers have even gone so far as to leave to their employees full latitude to arrange their working time as they please, so that each worker is free to fix his hours of work on his own, though subject to the conditions of notifying them in advance and of adhering to them strictly during a specified period. In point of fact, there is in principle nothing to prevent the worker from choosing a rigid schedule.

The system of flexible hours of work goes even further. Thanks to this system the workers are entirely free to arrange their working time as they wish, yet without being obliged to establish in advance the working hours that suit them. On the contrary, it is open to them to determine their time-table from day to day, the characteristic feature of the system of flexible hours of work being that the workers may distribute their hours as they wish at any time and without advance notice, though within certain limits.

This is an epoch-making development. Before the industrial era there were, of course, some relatively elastic arrangements of working time, with the employer fixing daily the hours to be worked. With the advent of mechanisation, however, these arrangements gave way not only to rules of diligence and punctuality in the interests of efficiency but also to rigid schedules of hours of work prescribed by the employer. Later on, when the paternalistic and authoritarian features of management began to fade, hours of work were fixed more and more frequently by common consent and even, in certain cases, by the workers alone, but without at first changing in any way the rigidity of arrangement of working time and the punctuality rule. Nowadays, however, these rules are increasingly losing their relevance to labour discipline, and current management trends are steadily reducing their importance, so that there is a return to flexible hours of work though they are fixed no longer by the employer but by the workers. Similar developments are occurring in respect of other aspects of work and of labour relations that are apt to cause tensions.

A recapitulation of the various points that have been made will show that a wide variety of systems can be considered:

A. Rigid arrangement of working time

1. Hours of work fixed rigidly for the undertaking as a whole by—
(a) the employer; or
(b) agreement between the employer and the workers.

2. Hours of work fixed rigidly for certains departments of the under-taking (staggering of working time) by—
(a) the employer; or
(b) agreement between the employer and the workers.

3. Hours of work fixed rigidly for the individual worker (with individual arrangement of working time) by—
(a) the employer;
(b) agreement between the employer and the worker concerned; or
(c) the individual worker.

B. Flexible arrangement of working time

Hours of work fixed from day to day by—

(*a*) the employer [1];

(*b*) the individual worker; or

(*c*) groups of workers.

LIMITATIONS AND RESTRICTIONS CONCERNING FLEXIBLE HOURS

Without entering into any detailed discussion of the meaning of the expression "flexible hours of work", it may be said here that it refers to a system under which individual workers are entitled, in principle, to arrange their daily working time as they like, day by day. In other words, the characteristic feature of the system is that it consists in a flexible daily distribution of hours to be worked.

In practice, however, this freedom of choice is restricted to a considerable extent by circumstances pertaining to the organisation of work and to the need to ensure communication between the members of the staff. The fact is that in most of the undertakings which apply the system of flexible hours of work, a certain stretch of time, which will be referred to as the period of compulsory attendance or "core time", is fixed during which each worker is required to attend. The period in question is specified in terms both of its duration and of its distribution over the working day. It may extend, for example, from 8 a.m. to 11.45 a.m. and from 2 p.m. to 4 p.m., which means that the daily duration of work cannot be less than five hours and three-quarters, the distribution of this minimum number of hours being specified. The system of flexible working hours makes it possible, in principle, to choose freely the times of starting and stopping work within set limits, as well as the number and distribution of hours worked over and above the prescribed minimum, that is, in other words, outside the period of compulsory attendance.

As has been indicated, the period of compulsory attendance marks the limits of the minimum daily number of hours of work. The number of hours worked in excess of that minimum is, however, also subject to limitations. One of them is laid down in the provisions of many labour laws relating to the maximum duration of a day's work and to compulsory breaks. Their purpose is to guarantee to the worker every day the breaks

---

[1] Today it is only rarely that hours of work are fixed from day to day by the employer; such cases occur especially in agriculture and in other sectors where the worker lives on the employer's premises.

that are physiologically essential for recuperation and rest. Where they are designed solely for that purpose, such statutory provisions are fully relevant to the case of flexible hours of work since the purpose is to prevent a worker from deliberately choosing a daily number of hours of work regarded as excessive from a physiological point of view; they provide the workers with some protection against any temptation to over-exert themselves. In principle, therefore, the workers are free to choose their daily hours of work within a time span having a minimum duration corresponding to the core time period and a maximum duration corresponding to the maximum number of daily hours of work laid down by law, including the prescribed breaks.

However, the number of hours of work can be extended up to the legal maximum only if the management provides the worker with the possibility of working throughout that time—that is, if the legal maximum is available. Yet the system of flexible hours of work in no way obliges the management to adopt working hours that will enable each member of its staff to choose a number of hours of work equal to the maximum daily number laid down by law, since that would oblige the undertaking to keep its doors open for an unduly long time, with resulting excessive costs. [1]

That is why undertakings which have adopted the system of flexible hours of work also generally place limits on the hours of operation of workshops or offices, in most cases by specifying the time at which work may begin at the earliest and the time at which it must end at the latest. The core time is usually divided into two parts so that the midday break may be freely chosen within certain limits. As a rule, labour legislation fixes the minimum duration of that break: thus except in the event of urgent work there may have to be a break of at least 30 minutes when the number of hours of work does not exceed nine and of at least 60 minutes when it does. In many cases the law also provides that the break must take place not later than after a certain lapse of time, for example five hours and a half.

Until recently, the employer was generally required by law to ensure observance of the breaks. He could undertake that responsibility by virtue of his right to lay down the daily timing and number of hours of work. He can no longer do so under the system of flexible hours of work since

---

[1] If the period of compulsory attendance stretched from 8 a.m. to 11.45 a.m. and from 2 p.m. to 4 p.m., that is, for five hours and three-quarters, and if the maximum daily duration of work amounted to 12 hours, including a break of one hour, the undertaking would have to remain open from 4 a.m. to 8 p.m.; if, for example, one of two workers having the same wish to work every day as long as possible wanted to finish work at 4 p.m. while the other wanted to begin work at 8 a.m., the former would have to arrive at 4 a.m. and the latter to leave at 8 p.m.

Flexible working hours

Figure 1. Example of flexible hours of work in a Swiss undertaking

6.30 a.m.	8.00 a.m.	11.45 a.m.	2.00 p.m.	4.00 p.m.	6.00 p.m.
Optional period	Core time	Optional period	Core time	Optional period	
Undertaking's working hours					

Undertaking's working hours: 6.30. a.m.— 6 p.m. = 11½ hours

Core time: 8 a.m.—11.45 a.m. = 3¾ hours
  2 p.m.— 4 p.m. = 2 hours
   = 5¾ hours

Period of optional attendance:
  Start of work between 6.30 a.m. and 8 a.m. ("Starting band")
  Midday break between 11.45 a.m. and 2 p.m.
  End of work between 4 p.m. and 6 p.m. ("Finishing band")

Midday break: the workers choose it individually between 11.45 a.m. and 2 p.m., taking into account the minimum breaks prescribed by law, namely 30 minutes if the number of hours of work does not exceed nine and 60 minutes if it does. As the midday break must occur, by law, not later than after five and a half hours of work, a worker who starts working as early as possible (6.30 a.m.) must take a break not later than at noon.

Minimum duration of work: 5¾ hours, which is the length of the core time.

Maximum duration of work: 10½ hours, that is, the undertaking's hours of opening less the minimum midday break of 60 minutes prescribed for that period of work.

---

he does not know for how long the workers intend to work nor at what time they intend to begin, so that there does not seem to be any way in which he could fix the necessary breaks for each day and for each member of the staff. It is thus up to the workers to abide by the statutorily required breaks as a counterpart to their entitlement to start and stop working when they please; the employer can be required only to fix the periods of compulsory attendance in such a way that the workers can comply with the provisions relating to the minimum duration of midday breaks.

It follows from the foregoing that the following conditions are of particular importance to the system of flexible hours of work:

(a) the span of the undertaking's working hours: the workers are required to choose their hours of work within that span, which must be appreciably longer than the core time and the prescribed hours of work since otherwise it would not be possible for the workers to distribute their own hours of work, that is, to arrange them flexibly;

(b) the core time or period of compulsory attendance: all the workers have to be present in the undertaking during that period, which determines the minimum duration of work and exercises an influence on the structure of all the individual work schedules;

(c) periods of optional attendance, often known as flexible time or the flexible hours: these periods comprise, in principle, the working hours of the undertaking that fall outside core time. It is during those hours (often known as "the starting and finishing bands") that a worker may choose every day when to start and stop working.

PRESCRIBED HOURS OF WORK AND MAKE-UP TIME

The hours of work provisions of laws, collective agreements or individual contracts generally refer not to the day but to the week or month. When they refer strictly to the day, the system of flexible working hours is not easy to apply because in that case it is possible to choose freely only the distribution of hours of work over the day, whereas day-to-day variations in the number of hours worked are excluded. The only normal requirement that is dropped is the obligation to be punctual, in the sense that it is no longer necessary to fix in advance the times of starting and stopping work daily.

On the basis of a prescribed weekly number of hours of work (44 for example), the distribution of working time can be easily varied, provided that the total number of hours worked over the week corresponds to the prescribed weekly number. In other words, the system of flexible hours of work presupposes that the actual and prescribed hours of work will tally at the latest within a week. If, therefore, the prescribed weekly number of hours is 44, as already mentioned by way of example, with a five-day week the average number of hours to be worked daily will be 8.8. It is, however, quite possible to work on certain days solely during the period of compulsory attendance and to make up on other days for the unworked hours by working during the optional period. Thus on the basis of the data shown in figure 1 the weekly period of work could be arranged as shown in table 1.

If a fixed number of hours must be worked every week, the possibilities of adjusting the daily number of hours of work at will are limited. If, for example, the actual hours worked are reduced at the beginning of the week, the optional periods will have to be used to the maximum towards the end of that week in order to make up the necessary amount of time, and during

11

Table 1. Possible distribution of hours actually worked under the system outlined in figure 1

Day	Core time	Optional period	Total
Monday	5¾	—	5¾
Tuesday	5¾	2¼	8
Wednesday	5¾	4¾	10½
Thursday	5¾	3½	9¼
Friday	5¾	4¾	10½

the last days of the week the worker would almost need a slide rule to make the actual hours of work tally with the prescribed hours.

Owing to these difficulties, many undertakings have adopted a system under which the number of hours to be worked is laid down only as a monthly total. Better use can then be made of the choices open, and the problems associated with make-up time, which can be a source of stress, arise only once a month.

There are, however, some other methods of making up time that are even more pliant. When the hours actually worked are calculated at the close of an accounting period, whether it be a week or a month, there may be some debit or credit hours, depending on whether the number of hours worked has been greater or smaller than the prescribed number; with the new methods it is generally possible, up to a certain point, to carry forward these credits and debits to the next accounting period, during which the process of offsetting can be carried out. This possibility of carry-over to the next accounting period increases the range of choice offered to the workers. Where, for example, a credit or debit of 10 hours may be carried forward, the monthly number of hours of work may vary from one month to another by up to 20 hours, as in the case in which a worker with a credit of 10 hours at the end of one month has a debit of 10 hours at the end of the next.

However, the credits and debits may not be carried forward indefinitely; there has to be some limit in the interests both of the worker and of the employer. In most cases the limit is fixed at between 10 and 20 hours; where it is fixed at 10 hours, any hours worked over and above that limit may not be made up or remunerated at the end of the month, while hours not worked up to that limit are subject to a corresponding reduction of pay and possibly also to disciplinary measures.

The purpose of this limitation is to prevent unreasonable workers from accumulating an excessive number of credit hours by choosing hours of work that are too long and consequently harmful to their health. It also provides some guarantee that over the long term there shall on the whole be compliance with the normal number of hours of work as laid down by law. There is also the point that for the employer the credits accumulated by the workers constitute debts that should be limited to a minimum. Conversely, by authorising a carry-over of debits, the employer pays in advance for work that has not yet been done; if such debits were carried over indefinitely, there could result substantial advances on pay, with the risk that they might be irrecoverably lost in the event of dismissals or voluntary departures of some members of the workforce.

The question of the number of credit and debit hours that may be authorised depends to some extent on the possibilities of returning to the norm. If the period of optional attendance is relatively short (or, in more technical language, "if the total bandwidth is restricted"), it might take a long time to make up a large debit or credit. Hence it is desirable to ensure that the optional period, the core time and the possibilities of carry-over are judiciously balanced.

There remains the likewise disputed question whether the use of credit during core time should also be authorised. Is it appropriate to allow workers whose hours of work are in credit to take whole days or half days off? Should one also go so far as to allow these supplementary holidays to be prolonged beyond the credit period provided that the permitted number of debit hours is not exceeded?

The solutions that have been adopted in practice up to now fall into three groups:

1. Core time is essentially a work period. Hence credit hours cannot be offset during that period and it is therefore not possible to take supplementary days off in respect of existing or future credits. Exceptions may be allowed in certain circumstances.

2. The credit hours may be utilised without any restriction during core time and even, if necessary, up to the level of permitted debits in the form of, for example—

(a) from half a day up to one day a month, provided that it is not added to a weekend; or

(b) from half a day to one day a month at any time of the week.

3. The credit hours accumulated during an accounting period may be used without restriction in the course of the following period.

The restrictions imposed on the use of credit hours during core time spring from the very nature of that period, during which all workers must be at work. That is why it is often laid down that in order to maintain the efficiency of the various departments of the undertaking, compensatory time

Table 2. Possible distribution of hours actually worked, with variations in the length of the working week, under a system of flexible hours of work without core time

Week	Number of hours actually worked	Prescribed hours of work	Credit or debit hours
First	$4 \times 10\frac{1}{2} = 42$	44	$- 2$
Second	$4 \times 10\frac{1}{2} = 42$	44	$- 4$
Third	$4 \times 10\frac{1}{2} = 42$	44	$- 6$
Fourth	$4 \times 10\frac{1}{2} = 42$	44	$- 8$
Fifth	$4 \times 10\frac{1}{2} = 42$	44	-10
Sixth	$5 \times 10\frac{1}{2} = 52\frac{1}{2}$	44	$- 1\frac{1}{2}$

off may not be taken during core time except with the agreement of the supervisor.

However, these restrictions also have the purpose of preventing a diminution of the weekly number of hours of work coupled with an increase in the daily number, because if there were complete freedom in this respect a daily number of hours of work corresponding to the maximum number would virtually result in a four-day week. In an extreme instance of the case that has been selected for purposes of illustration, hours of work could be arranged in the way shown in table 2.

Such an arrangement of hours of work would not be consistent, however, with the purpose of the system of flexible working hours and, owing to the frequency of days of ten and a half hours, would lead inevitably to an excessive call on the workers' health and mental faculties, and consequently to a diminution in the undertaking's production capacity.

Moreover, if the use of credit hours served only to prolong the weekend holiday, the working of the undertaking might be gravely upset not only on the Monday but also and especially on the Friday afternoon, for it might happen that as from that afternoon half the staff, if not more, would be absent. It is indeed for that reason that, as has already been noted, many undertakings which in principle allow credit hours to be taken in the form of supplementary days off expressly forbid the adding of these days to the weekend holiday, or authorise it only in exceptional circumstances.

ABSENCES

With flexible hours of work there has to be a system for determining, whether by the workers themselves or independently of them, the hours of attendance in the undertaking. Hours of attendance are not identical with the remunerated hours: on the one hand, any time that is required to be worked outside the undertaking is generally included in the hours of attendance, while on the other hand it is necessary to record the hours which, though not actually worked, must be paid for by law or under the terms of a collective agreement or the rules of the undertaking (for example, holidays or absences due to sickness or accidents).

Hours worked outside the undertaking

Among the occupational activities carried on outside the usual place of work, reference may be made to travel on business, authorised attendance at courses or meetings for technical training or general education, appointments with customers and suppliers and participation in technical exhibitions. As a rule it is not necessary to record brief absences for occupational reasons falling within the working day and in respect of which any special rule would be superfluous. As for fairly long absences, it is usual to credit the person concerned daily with the prescribed daily number of hours in respect not only of the hours worked but also of the time spent on business travel and entertaining. In many cases credit is given even for a number of hours greater than the prescribed daily number of hours of work up to the maximum number of hours of opening the undertaking less the midday break. If the beginning or end of a day's hours of work is spent outside the usual place of work during an absence required for business purposes, then sometimes the number of hours worked is brought up to the prescribed number while sometimes only the hours that are worked within the limits of optional attendance (i.e. the starting or finishing band) are treated as hours worked. Another possibility is to have a theoretical schedule and to regard as hours worked absences for occupational reasons falling within the times specified in the schedule.

These various indications show that it is not easy to assess absences for occupational reasons; hence it is necessary to include detailed provisions in that regard in the rules, or to deal with each case separately.

Absences paid for

For the purposes of a system of flexible hours of work, it is necessary to define exactly the absences that are to be paid for as time worked. Under the law or under collective agreements, the absences in question are those for annual holidays, public holidays, sickness or accident or for complying with certain legal obligations such as military service, but they also include absences which are often authorised under the rules of undertakings for such events as house removals, decease or funeral of a near relation, marriage or the birth of a child.

Absences for the whole day or half a day that must be paid for by law or by contract or under a collective agreement or an undertaking's rules are reckoned on the basis of the prescribed working day. This method has become general, no doubt because it corresponds to the sense of rules relating to absences paid for. It is more difficult to deal with shorter absences, that is of only a few hours. If these absences are regarded as lawful, they must be treated as hours worked, and be paid for accordingly. When they fall within the period of compulsory attendance, their definition is clear and straightforward. When, however, they fall within the period of optional attendance they may be treated as working time sometimes up to the limit of the prescribed daily hours of work and sometimes only to the extent that they fall within the limits of the theoretical schedule. These two limitations are often combined. Clear rules concerning short absences are necessary in order to prevent a worker who, for instance, had to leave work in the middle of an afternoon because of an industrial accident from claiming that it had been his intention to attend on that day throughout the optional period. Absences paid for must be limited on both sides: they cannot be extended at the cost of the undertaking up to the maximum possible number of hours of work (core time plus the whole optional period), nor can they be restricted by the management to the minimum number of hours of work (core time).

Unpaid absences

As a rule, absences for reasons other than those that have been indicated are not paid for. They include in particular interruptions of work for personal reasons (e.g. consulting a doctor in cases of mild illness, shopping, private visiting) but also absences due to the breakdown of a means of transport or to traffic congestion. Unpaid absences must fall within the period of optional attendance. Permission is therefore not necessary since the worker can decide himself whether he intends to work during the period in question. On the other hand, unpaid absences during the period of compulsory attendance are in general not allowed; they may be authorised by a supervisor by way of exception provided that they are subsequently made up for during the period of optional attendance. Unpaid absences that are not authorised are treated as such and, in general, cannot be made up for from credit hours.

OVERTIME

When the number of daily hours of work is fixed, it is fairly easy to define overtime work as all work carried out outside those hours, and to credit it accordingly. On the other hand, where there is a system of flexible hours of work a new definition is needed in order to distinguish between overtime work proper, which must be paid for at a higher rate, and extra time worked in order to amass credit hours or to make up for debit hours. Since overtime pay sometimes represents a high proportion of the workers' earnings, this distinction is as important to the undertaking as it is to the workers.

Whatever the particular definition adopted, only work that has been expressly required in advance by the supervisor can be regarded as overtime since it is only in exceptional cases that a supervisor is entitled to confirm *a posteriori* that a particular job has been carried out as overtime work. This, however, does not solve the problem. What has to be avoided is that the workers, by adjusting their hours of daily work, should practically force their supervisors to require overtime, to be paid for at an increased rate. On the other hand the management should not be enabled to avoid increased payment for overtime work by parrying temporary fluctuations in the volume of work through periods of optional attendance.

It is clearly out of the question that every hour of work that has been required over and above core time should be paid for at an increased overtime rate, since the workers would then be able to transform the period of optional attendance into overtime: if they worked for a while solely during core time they would, of course, incur heavy debits of hours and consequential deductions from their pay; but in normal circumstances the management would soon be forced to oblige them to work during the periods of optional hours in order to keep the undertaking running smoothly. So long as wage deductions due to unacceptable debit hours of work (that is, those exceeding the authorised limit of 10 to 20 hours) are not increased to the same extent as are the wages paid for overtime, it is not possible to treat unreservedly as overtime all the hours that have to be worked outside core time.

All these points are at the basis of two systems governing overtime:

1. Under the first of these systems, overtime work that has been required is paid for at a higher rate only when the workers concerned have worked the prescribed number of hours during the accounting period. If they have not, and have therefore marked up a debit of hours, the overtime that they were required to work serves first of all to offset that debit, whereupon only the hours worked in excess of the prescribed number are regarded as attracting an increased rate of pay.

This system encourages the workers to abide by the prescribed number of hours of work during the accounting period, with the result that overtime retains its traditional sense of referring to hours worked over and above the prescribed number.

Table 3. Examples of computation of overtime and carry-over of hours worked in cases in which overtime offsets debits in ordinary hours worked

Item	Worker				
	A	B	C	D	E
Hours actually worked, including five required hours of overtime	175	175	185	185	170
Credit or debit hours carried forward from the preceding month	+4	−4	+4	−4	−7
	179	171	189	181	163
Prescribed hours of work	176	176	176	176	176
Balance [1]	+3	−5	+13	+5	−13[2]
Overtime hours paid for at a higher rate	3	0	5	5	0
New balance carried forward to the next month	0	−5	+8	0	−10

[1] The five hours of required overtime work are payable at an increased rate up to the amount of this balance if it is positive. [2] As this balance is negative, there is no question of paying for the overtime at an increased rate. Since a debit of only ten hours can be carried forward, payment for the remaining three hours is deducted from the wage.

The way in which overtime is calculated under this system can be seen from the examples given in table 3.

2. Under the second system, payment for overtime and payment for hours worked during the optional period are calculated separately, and the increased rate of payment for overtime is granted irrespective of the credit or debit hours. The hours of overtime work are, however, defined in a restrictive sense: only hours required to be worked over and above the prescribed daily hours of work are regarded as overtime and paid for at an increased rate. For example, if the prescribed daily number of hours of work is 8.8, only required hours that oblige the person concerned to work beyond that limit can be regarded as entitling to an increase in pay. On the other hand if workers do only 7½ hours they can be required to work 1.3 hours more without increased payment. In other cases a theoretical schedule of working hours is laid down which may run, for example, from 8 a.m. to noon and from 1 p.m. to 5.48 p.m. In such a case, only hours worked outside that schedule, i.e. before 8 a.m. and after 5.48 p.m., are regarded as overtime and payable at an increased rate. On the basis of the same assumptions as in the case of the first series of examples, the situation works out as shown in table 4.

As can be seen from these two series of examples, the results vary with the method employed. In any case, however, the workers have the possibility of ensuring that any overtime hours which they may be required to work shall be paid for at an increased rate. Under the first method, they must

Table 4. Examples of computation of overtime and carry-over of hours worked in cases in which overtime does not offset debits in ordinary hours worked

Item	Worker				
	A	B	C	D	E
Hours actually worked, excluding overtime	170	170	180	180	165
Credit or debit hours carried forward from the preceding month	+4	−4	+4	−4	−7
	174	166	184	176	158
Prescribed hours of work	176	176	176	176	176
Balance carried forward to the next month	−2	−10	+8	0	−18[1]
Overtime hours to be paid for at an increased rate [2]	5	5	5	5	5

[1] Since the debit for worker E amounts to 18 hours, that worker's wage is reduced by the amount of remuneration for 8 hours because a debit of only 10 hours may be carried forward to the next month.
[2] These are overtime hours falling outside the theoretical schedule or which have been worked over and above the prescribed 8.8 daily hours of work.

see to it that the number of their credit hours is equal to or exceeds the number of required overtime hours. Under the second method they will endeavour to work the prescribed daily number of hours whenever they are required to work overtime. This method nevertheless makes the situation of worker E uncertain: because he has a debit of 18 hours, only 10 of which may be carried forward, his wage will be reduced by the equivalent of payment for eight hours, but he will nevertheless be paid at an increased rate for five hours of overtime work.

Both methods enable workers, at their request, to offset overtime with time off. There are, however, various ways in which this principle is applied. According to some rules, the offsetting is at a ratio of 1 to 1. According to others, a credit in hours is awarded which increases pro rata with the increase in payment for the overtime worked, while yet others provide that, unlike the case with credits carried forward, the credit in overtime may be offset by means of whole days of time off.

The rules relating to overtime have to be in strict accordance with the provisions of the law and of collective agreements. Inasmuch as those provisions often vary widely with the country and even from one industry to another within the same country, only a few illustrations can be given here of practices that have been adopted; no opinion is expressed on their merits.

ANTICIPATORY OR RETROACTIVE OFFSETTING OF WORKLESS DAYS

In various countries labour legislation authorises undertakings to suspend work entirely for specified reasons (and in any case with the workers' consent) on certain days, and to make up for those days, either in advance or retroactively, with corresponding work time over a certain period. This compensating time is not treated as overtime entitling to an increase in wage rates. It can take the form of an increase in the prescribed number of hours of work or in the period of compulsory attendance during a certain lapse of time and even, where necessary, throughout the year. Such time can also be regarded as simply a debt to be repaid, whether in advance or subsequently, with credit hours. In that event, however, care must be taken in certain cases to ensure that the methods of carrying forward the credits or debits are sufficiently flexible.

ILLUSTRATIONS DRAWN FROM THE RULES OF SELECTED UNDERTAKINGS

The illustrations given below are drawn from the rules of various undertakings in the Swiss engineering and electrical industry; similar provisions could be found in the internal rules of establishments in other industries.

A. Hours of work

Prescribed number of hours of work

With a 44-hour week spread over five days, the average daily number of hours of work is 8.8. The standard number of hours of work is determined as follows :
Monday-Friday daily average 8.8 hours:
i.e. monthly with 20 work days 176.0 hours;
i.e. monthly with 21 work days 184.8 hours;
i.e. monthly with 22 work days 193.6 hours and so on.
Whenever necessary, the personnel department ascertains the prescribed monthly number of hours of work and posts it up near the apparatus recording the hours of attendance.

Core time

The core time during which all members of the staff must normally be at work is as follows:
8 a.m. to 11.42 a.m. = 3.7 hours
2 p.m. to 4 p.m.   = 2   hours
          Total   = 5.7 hours

Period of optional attendance

The period of optional attendance during which hours of work can be individually selected, subject to compliance with the statutory standards concerning the maximum daily number of hours of work including the prescribed minimum breaks, is as follows:
Work starts between 6.30 a.m. and 8 a.m.
Midday break between 11.42 a.m. and 2 p.m.
Work finishes between 4 p.m. and 6 p.m.
(not later than 5 p.m. on the eve of a public holiday).
Hours of attendance recorded outside the periods of optional or compulsory attendance, that is, before 6.30 a.m. and after 8 p.m., are not taken into account

(except in the case of required overtime work) in the wage payment or in marking up the credit hours of the person concerned.

Recapitulation of statutory provisions relating to hours of work

The provisions of labour law as well as all other legal provisions relating to hours of work must be complied with in all circumstances.

(a) *Maximum number of hours of work*

— for adults: 11.2 hours a day, including overtime but with a maximum of 50 hours a week not including overtime;
— for young people up to completion of their nineteenth year: nine hours a day, including overtime and/or the hours made up for in advance;
— for apprentices up to completion of their twentieth year: nine hours a day, including overtime and/or the hours made up for in advance.

(b) *Minimum breaks*

When work is uninterrupted for—
more than seven hours: a minimum uninterrupted break of half an hour;
more than nine hours: breaks totalling 1 hour, including an uninterrupted half-hour.

The midday break must be fitted in not later than after five and a half hours of work.

Number of hours actually worked and balance of hours

The monthly number of hours actually worked must correspond on the average to the prescribed number.

Differences between *the number of hours actually worked*
$\pm$ a positive or negative balance from the preceding month,
$+$ any absences paid for,
$-$ any overtime paid for separately

and *the prescribed number of hours of work* are tolerated up to a maximum balance of $\pm$ 10 hours at the end of the month.

Any cumulative difference, excluding overtime, is taken into account up to the tolerated limit and is—

(*a*) communicated to the worker on his pay slip (positive balance $=$ credit hours; negative balance $=$ debit hours); and

(*b*) carried forward to the next month.

In the event of overstepping of the threshold of tolerance, the following rules apply:

(*a*) credit hours in excess of ten at the end of the month are discounted without compensation; and

(*b*) debit hours in excess of ten at the end of the month
   (i) entail a corresponding reduction of pay in the next month; and
   (ii) are reported to the appropriate supervisor.

In the event of expiry of the contract, the worker is required to make up for any balance of hours of work up to the time of his departure.

As a rule the worker is required every month to complete a number of hours equal to the prescribed number. A difference of up to $\pm$ ten hours of optional time is nevertheless tolerated and must be carried forward to the next month. This carry-over must be calculated afresh every month. It should be noted in this connection that—

(*a*) the credit that may be carried forward may not exceed ten hours of work; and

(*b*) a debit exceeding ten hours of work can entail a wage reduction.

B. Restrictions

The workers' right to begin and end work when they please may be wholly or partially restricted by—

(a) the exclusion from enjoyment of that right of certain members of the staff (belonging to specified departments or groups) if necessary for technical reasons relating to the organisation, running and supervision of operations or when the volume of work fluctuates;

(b) special provisions of a general or sectoral character or agreements relating to special cases, overtime, etc.;

(c) voluntary agreements between supervisors and subordinates or among certain workers in cases of work in groups, meetings, etc.; and

(d) withdrawal from certain workers of continued enjoyment of the advantages of the system of flexible working hours on the ground that they have misused it.

C. Absenteeism and absences

Where an undertaking has rules relating to absences, it is fairly easy to comply with their provisions:

All absences are subject to the provisions of the rules.

Absences of a whole day or half a day must be notified, if possible in advance, to the appropriate supervisor and recorded. Absences that under the rules are paid for and treated as hours worked are reckoned at the rate of 8.8 hours per day or 4.4 hours per half-day. Unpaid holidays of a whole day or half a day must be expressly authorised by the supervisors. They are treated as unworked hours and may not be offset with hours worked during the period of optional attendance.

Very short absences during core time are paid for only if they are—

(a) defined in the rules relating to absences or in special instructions as entitling to remuneration; and

(b) justified on the attendance card, with an indication of the appropriate code number.

Unpaid short absences during core time are treated as unworked hours and may not be offset with hours of work during the period of optional attendance.

Short absences during the optional period do not have to be justified and are not paid for. They may be offset with hours worked during that period.

Short absences which, according to the rules, may be paid for even during the period of optional attendance refer solely to hours falling within the limits of the theoretical work day (running from 7.45 a.m. at the earliest to 5.00 p.m. at the latest) provided that they do not exceed the prescribed duration of a day's work, that is, 8.8 hours.

In an undertaking that does not have any special rules, absences have to be defined in much greater detail, as the following example shows.

Absences

1. *Outside duties*

(a) *Definition.* Time spent on outside duties is time worked outside the plant for the purpose of . . . (for example, calling on customers and suppliers, repairs, etc.).

(b) *Outside duties of a whole day or half a day.* Absence on outside duties is reckoned as follows in terms of hours of work:

1 whole day = 8.8 hours;
½ day = 4.4 hours.

(c) *Outside duties involving leaving the plant during the morning and returning during the afternoon.* In this case the hours reckoned as worked during the normal period of attendance are those spent between leaving the plant during the morning and returning during the afternoon less a deduction of one hour's break.

(d) *Outside duties involving leaving during the afternoon without returning on the same day.* In this case the hours reckoned as worked during the normal period of attendance are those spent between leaving the plant and completion of the work outside the plant.

(e) *Travel and going out with visitors* (sales and development engineers, buyers, etc.):

(i) midday meal with a visitor. This case is dealt with as under (c).

(ii) going out in the afternoon to dine and spend the evening with a visitor. In this case, the period of attendance at the plant is increased up to a maximum of 8.8 hours per day.

(iii) journeys of a whole day or half a day. The period of attendance is reckoned as 8.8 hours in the case of a journey lasting a whole day and of 4.4 hours in the case of a journey lasting half a day.

(iv) leaving during the morning or during the afternoon to go on a journey. In these cases the period of attendance at the plant is increased up to a maximum of 8.8 hours per day.

(v) return from a journey during the day. In this case, too, the period of attendance at the plant from the moment of arrival of the person concerned is increased up to a maximum of 8.8 hours per day.

2. Vocational training

(a) *Whole day or half a day of vocational training.* Detachment to a course, seminar, lecture, etc., is reckoned at 8.8 hours for a whole day and 4.4 hours for half a day.

(b) *Break during the day for vocational training.* Where a person who is appointed to attend a course, seminar, lecture, etc., has to leave his work during the day, the time of attendance at the plant is increased up to a maximum of 8.8 hours per day.

(c) *Evening classes.* Workers taking evening classes may claim one hour of normal attendance for each evening on which they go to the classes (whatever the time at which the classes begin). [1]

3. Time off with pay

Time off with pay is granted to the staff in respect of the following circumstances: house removal, wedding of a colleague, birth of a legitimate child, decease of a near relative, inspection of the weapons and equipment of persons liable for military service.

This time off is reckoned as normal attendance at the rate of 8.8 hours per whole day and 4.4 hours per half day.

Time off is granted by the department head in accordance with rules jointly established by the employers' and workers' organisations that are parties to the general collective agreement for the metal trades.

---

[1] Similar compensatory arrangements (4.4 hours of normal attendance) are made in respect of Saturdays worked to make up for the closing of the undertaking between Christmas and New Year's day.

4. Accidents and sickness

(a) *Absences of a whole day or half a day.* In these cases the hours reckoned as normal hours of attendance are 8.8 hours per whole day and 4.4 hours per half-day.

(b) *Absences during the day with or without return to the plant on the same day.* The time of attendance at the plant is increased up to a maximum of 8.8 hours per day for persons who leave their work, whether or not they return on the same day.

5. Military service

Absences on compulsory military service are paid for up to one month a year. The hours are reckoned as follows: 8.8 hours per whole day, 4.4 hours per half-day.

6. Holidays

Within the limits of their individual rights to holidays, staff members may take holidays authorised by the department head. The hours are reckoned as follows: 8.8 hours per whole day, 4.4 hours per half-day. All workers taking holidays must ensure that they keep available the number of days corresponding to the annual two-week closure of the plant, i.e. 10 working days.

7. Compensatory time off of half a day

Time off of half a day offsetting credit hours may be authorised once a month by the department head.

8. Absences for odd hours

(a) *Absences during optional working time.* No reason need be given for absences during the period of optional working hours.

(b) *Absences during core time.* Absences during core time are to be avoided, but may be authorised in an emergency by the immediate supervisor and as a rule are not reckoned as hours worked.

9. Authorisations and attendance card

(a) *Foreseeable absences.* As a rule, all absences in respect of holidays with pay (rule 4.3) or without, military service, medical treatment, etc., must be authorised in advance and the attendance card endorsed accordingly by the department head.

(b) *Unforeseeable absences.* In all cases of unforeseeable absence (accident, sickness, sudden decease of a relative, etc.), the attendance card must be endorsed by the department head as a check and a sign of approval.

D. Overtime

Hours worked at the direct request of the supervisor over and above the normal daily number of hours of work are regarded as overtime entitling to increased pay.

Alternatively:

Only hours worked at the direct request of the supervisor are regarded as constituting overtime. They are paid for at an increased rate only in as far as they exceed the prescribed monthly number of hours of work, account being taken of the balance of optional hours of work carried forward from the preceding month.

Overtime worked at the supervisor's request may be offset on demand at a ratio of 1 to 1 by absences or supplementary days off.

E. Offsetting credit hours

Only in exceptional cases and subject to the prior authorisation of the supervisor may a worker with credit hours have leave of absence for up to half a day per month during the period of compulsory attendance.

F. Attendance records

In view of the possibility of modifying the hours worked every day, it is necessary to register the hours of attendance of all members of the staff. They are recorded for each individual staff member by means of special apparatus. Registering for other persons is regarded as fraudulent and is punished accordingly.

Every staff member is issued with an attendance card on which the times of—

(a) starting work,

(b) beginning and ending the midday break,

(c) stopping work, and

(d) interruptions of work

must be indicated by means of the apparatus provided for the staff member's sector of work. The time clocks mark the times to one-hundredth of an hour.

Handwritten entries of hours and decimal fractions of hours in respect of occupational activities carried on outside the usual place of work, training courses, absences and overtime must be made in accordance with the «instructions relating to the administration of flexible hours of work».

ORIGINS AND DEVELOPMENT OF THE SYSTEM

2

It is no longer possible today to identify the inventor of the system of flexible hours of work in its present form. All that is certain is that the system had long been practised here and there before becoming a topic of serious discussion and before it received its present designation.

It should be recalled, moreover, that, at a time when the method of distribution of hours of work was as rigorous as it was rigid, heads of undertakings did not necessarily feel obliged to apply strictly the fixed hours of work: it very often happened that the management of an undertaking did not allow the senior staff to separate their working time strictly from their leisure time so that, in many cases, the hours which they worked greatly exceeded any official schedule; and it was in any case possible for the employer, as the boss, to arrange working time as he pleased both for himself and for his subordinates. As the functions of management became more complex, there was an increase in the number of persons in the undertaking who were more or less free to arrange their own hours of work and who thereby also contributed to some loosening of the schedule.

Furthermore, for many years past a good many highly qualified and particularly zealous employees have no longer felt obliged to show extreme punctuality in starting and ending their day's work. In many cases they went on working on certain days until well after the undertaking's closing time because they wanted to finish a job or because they were well disposed towards the undertaking and consequently had their work at heart, or again because they were so absorbed in their work that they lost their sense of time. Some of them arrived in the morning before opening time because they wanted to finish a job in time or because, for personal reasons, they had left for work earlier than usual, and so on. Of course these diligent workers might sometimes take the liberty of arriving a little later in the morning and of leaving earlier, or of sometimes interrupting their work during the day to suit their convenience. Sensible heads of personnel generally tolerated these small infringements of the official hours of work because they considered that, from the point of view of the undertaking, the work performed was more important than the number of hours worked during the official hours provided that there were no effects on the undertaking as a whole and no disturbances of its work.

It also often happened that the rigid work schedule was called in question owing to the unpunctuality of some of the staff and to the frequency of individual requests for authorisation to arrive occasionally late at work or to leave work before due time in order to deal with urgent personal matters. These departures from the rule were also, in general, tacitly accepted, especially when the labour market was particularly constricted, provided that the unworked hours were, in principle, subsequently made up by those concerned.

Thus well before there was any question of a system of flexible working hours, the arrangement of working time was in practice often loosened and adjusted up to a point. It seems possible, therefore, that a number of undertakings, acting independently of each other, had already sought to formalise and systematise the above-mentioned departures from the norm.

It was, it seems, only in 1967 that flexible hours of work as an efficient system of distribution of working time first became a topic of general public discussion. Though some similar experiments had previously been made, they were not of any decisive significance, whereas in 1967 the Bölkow company (Messerschmitt-Bölkow-Blohm GmbH) at Ottobrunn in the Federal Republic of Germany introduced the system of flexible working hours for a comparatively large proportion of its workforce. [1] In subsequent years the new system became the subject of lively discussion, especially in the Federal Republic of Germany, among those concerned with personnel administration and with scientific management.

The principle on which it was based thus gained acceptance to such an extent that according to Schott the number of undertakings and government departments which had introduced the system, and which had already numbered some two to three hundred in April 1970, had risen to some two thousand by August 1971. According to estimates made by the Deutsche Industrieinstitut, the system applied at the end of 1971 to about 2 per cent of all workers. Even though a forecast made in 1972 that the system would

---

[1] See R. Schott: "Arbeitswissenschaftliche Fragen an eine variable Arbeitszeit", in *Arbeit und Leistung* (Frechen-Köln), No. 6, 1972; J. Harvey Bolton: *Flexible working hours* (Wembley, Middlesex, Anbar Publications, 1971); Jean-François Baudraz: *L'horaire variable de travail* (Paris, Les Editions d'organisation, 1973); Stephen J. Baum and W. McEwan Young: *A practical guide to flexible working hours* (London, Kogan Page, 1973).

have been adopted by 1975 by one half of all the undertakings in the Federal Republic of Germany might prove to have been too optimistic, the facts nevertheless show clearly that the system has made a great deal of headway. Among Swiss undertakings it was the firm of Landis and Gyr AG at Zug which, in 1969, was the first to take the initiative of introducing the system of flexible working hours. Since then the system has spread with astonishing speed, especially in industry and among private undertakings in the services sector. [1] Although official data and statistics are not available, it seems that Switzerland is at present ahead of all other countries in this field: according to private estimates, over 30 per cent of all workers in that country today work under the new system.

Experiments with flexible working hours became increasingly widespread; sometimes they were carried out at the request of the authorities, as for example in France [2], and sometimes the initiative came from within interested undertakings and organisations. In nearly all the industrialised countries of Europe there are today undertakings which apply the system or are planning to do so: in addition to the Federal Republic of Germany and Switzerland, mention may be made of the United Kingdom, the Scandinavian countries, the Benelux countries, France, Italy and Spain. [3] Many undertakings have also gone over to flexible working hours in the United States, Canada, Japan and Australia. Almost everywhere enhanced interest in flexible working hours has been shown since the Organisation for Economic Co-operation and Development held a conference on new patterns of working time in Paris from 26 to 29 September 1972.

In the course of the past two or three years there have been countless scientific studies and factual reports on flexible working hours. Although comprehensive descriptions of the expansion of the new system in the world as a whole or even in particular countries are still lacking, it is plain that it has very rapidly gone beyond the experimental phase. It has shown itself to be a thoroughly practicable way of arranging working hours, and in essentials seems bound to become permanently established, at any rate in highly important sectors of the economy. The extent to which it will make further progress will depend, of course, on broad structural and environmental circumstances, and above all on the workers' preferences and needs.

---

[1] "Expérience avec l'horaire mobile de travail", in *Journal des Associations patronales suisses* (Zurich), 66th Year, No. 7, 18 Feb. 1971, pp. 149-152; No. 8, 25 Feb. 1971, pp. 171-173; and No. 9, 4 Mar. 1971, pp. 193-195.

[2] J. de Chalendar: *L'aménagement des temps de travail au niveau de la journée: L'horaire variable ou libre*, Rapport du groupe d'études réuni à la demande du Premier Ministre (Paris, *La documentation française*, 1972).

[3] Alvar O. Elbing, Herman Gadon and John R. M. Gordon: "Flexible working hours: It's about time", in *Harvard Business Review*, Jan.-Feb. 1974, p. 18.

When the pioneering Messerschmitt-Bölkow-Blohm firm at Ottobrunn adopted the system of flexible working hours, it was obviously motivated above all by considerations of individual psychology. In this connection, the following passage from an important article seems worth quoting [1]:

At Ottobrunn the introduction of the system of flexible working hours was not prompted by any particular concern to shorten the commuting time of the staff by means of a new distribution of hours of work, nor by the daily traffic difficulties on access roads to the factory and in parking lots due to the simultaneous arrival and departures of many vehicles, nor even by desire on the part of the undertaking to obtain from its staff credit hours, which, for that matter, it subsequently did obtain in large measure; it was prompted primarily by the fact that many workers had shown themselves to be increasingly disinclined to put up with a situation in which the undertaking, while ready enough to accept night work that had not been expressly required at the close of the scheduled hours of work because this suited it at a time when its operations were in full swing, did not as a rule tolerate any delay on the following morning in starting work under the same schedule, however justified such a delay might have seemed to the workers. It was thus solely a problem of staff management. A novel aspect of what happened now was that instead of facing that situation with resignation and either yielding or putting up a silent resistance as had been the habit for generations, the workers made it plain to the management that they were disgruntled; and another novel aspect was that the management itself did not play the problem down, and that in terms of personnel management it did not resort to harsh measures but sought rather to go to the root of the problem and to arrive at a solution in full conformity with the interests of the undertaking.

According to the principle of punctuality, which is the necessary corollary of any rigid arrangement of working hours, there should have been strict compliance by the workers with the time fixed for the end of a day's work. Several cases could be mentioned, however, of undertakings which accordingly decided that the whole of their staff, including office personnel, had to leave their work not later than 30 minutes after the official closing time of workshops and offices, and which met with little understanding, so that they were obliged in the long run to tolerate certain departures from the rule in order to take account of individual work habits and to stimulate their workers' application to their tasks.

For some other undertakings, the system of flexible working hours was adopted in order to give formal sanction to an existing state of affairs. Either from a concern to practise a more effective personnel policy or because of the pressure of a constricted labour market, a growing number of employers had come to tolerate late arrivals and early departures, provided that the time lost was offset in advance or subsequently. Other employers, however, remained totally uncompromising in that respect, thereby giving

---

[1] Alfred Hillert: "Gleitende Arbeitszeit als Instrument der Personalführung", in *Personalführung* (Düsseldorf), No. 10, 1972, p. 190.

rise to grudges and envy among their staff, since supervision and control, especially so far as individual offsetting of unworked hours was concerned, became increasingly unreal. Thus the introduction of the system of flexible working hours put an end to the uncertainties concerning the acceptability of ad hoc individual arrangements of hours of work, inasmuch as the rules of punctuality were completely abandoned in respect of some part of the working day.

Attitudes such as those that have been mentioned were no doubt more decisive than the pressures inseparable from any transport policy. In the cases of public transport and of private vehicles used for business purposes, the problems caused by the peak hours of traffic (including those arising at the hours of departure and arrival in the parking lots belonging to undertakings) might in theory be more easily dealt with through a co-ordinated local staggering of work schedules than by the adoption of the system of flexible working hours; if imposed by the authorities, such a staggering would make it possible during the rush hours to spread out and distribute, with maximum effectiveness in accordance with the volume of traffic, the arrivals and departures of vehicles used to commute to and from work. However, the co-ordination of the staggering of hours of work is all too often left to the judgement of each employer, so that it is scarcely ever of any benefit to the categories of workers in greatest need of travel facilities. So long as that is so the system of flexible working hours at least affords an improvement on the chaotic traffic situation which tends to result from inadequate co-ordination of the work schedules of different undertakings.

Owing to the condition of the labour market, many undertakings have in recent years adjusted their work schedules in a variety of ways to all kinds of well grounded individual desiderata. As a result, there has come about in certain cases a very wide diversity in the time scheduled as the beginning of the working day. Such a state of affairs very quickly leads to confusion and to feelings of resentment due to the fact that some workers or categories of workers are, or are thought to be, favoured; and it also leads to a diminution in the undertaking's production capacity during the hours of arrival and departure as long as the fiction of fixed hours of work subject to exceptions is maintained despite the fact that exceptions have long been the rule.

Originally it was probably practical reasons of this kind coupled with a concern to take into account individual attitudes and the principles of efficient management that were uppermost in the minds of most of the employers who were prepared to consider introducing the system of flexible hours of work. The relationship between this system, on the one hand,

and the two main types of need identified in the theory of motivation, namely the human need for respect and appreciation and the aspiration towards self-fulfilment, was fully grasped only after a more detailed analysis. It was only gradually that emphasis was placed on the importance to the workers of the possibility of exercising freedom of choice in a new field at a time when their lives were being subjected to an increasing number of material constraints. In other words, the theory on which the system of flexible working hours is based was perceived not at the start but only when the wide implications of the new system came to be understood; though in this field as in others it is often difficult to decide whether the theory may not have been put well forward as a kind a banner floating over all other considerations of a practical or organisational nature, or pertaining to the labour market, the physiology of work and industrial psychology. Whatever may have been the motives of its promoters, however, the system of flexible working hours is now more than a fashionable gimmick: within a short space of time it has established itself as a technique whose advantages and drawbacks merit impartial examination.

ADVANTAGES AND DRAWBACKS

3

Both in what has been written on the subject and among persons currently using the system it is claimed that flexible working hours are advantageous both to the workers and to employers, the general opinion thus being that neither are losers as a result of the introduction of the system. Nevertheless, not only is it difficult to draw up a balance sheet for each party; it is even quite impossible to assess the advantages in quantitative terms for purposes of comparison inasmuch as there are, on the one hand, non-quantifiable gains in freedom for the workers and, on the other, employers' aims that could be summed up, though not in all circumstances, as relating to increased productivity.

FUNDAMENTALS

It is clear that underlying the system of flexible working hours there are well defined mental attitudes. On the part of the employer, apart from a favourable attitude towards worker participation in the running of the undertaking, it requires recognition of the worker's mental maturity and free will; but it also requires on the part of the workers a willingness to co-operate, loyalty, and a clear sense of their responsibilities towards the undertaking as a whole, so that their independence with regard to the distribution of hours of work and the corresponding restrictions of their supervisors' authority shall not lead to internal strife, disintegration and chaos.

The system of flexible working hours thus presupposes a co-operative management of affairs. Save in exceptional and objectively defined cases, management sees its prerogatives dwindling to the extent that the personnel benefits from greater freedom: the scope for authoritarian management thus shrinks. If, however, subordinates do not assume the greater responsibilities which the proper working of the undertaking requires, the advantages of the system of flexible working hours ultimately prove illusory both for the staff and for the employer.

The new system generally entails a breakup of firmly established structures, making it necessary to appoint substitutes, if only temporarily, with delegated powers, to institutionalise agreements among the members of the same team, and to multiply informal contacts between groups of workers. This implies a wider diffusion of information and a general decentralisation of decision-making powers so that relatively small units working independently shall be able in the absence of their supervisors to go on functioning normally and to contribute to the proper working of all parts of the undertaking consistently with common aims. If the system of flexible working hours did not have as its corollary management principles of the kind that have been indicated, its drawbacks would in all likelihood be greater than its advantages.

Furthermore, flexible working hours oblige supervisors at all levels to prepare and plan work in such a manner that each team can know in good time what has to be done and when. Hence the staff at all senior levels must be particularly well qualified, because without proper planning the system of flexible working hours leads to a waste of time which causes discontent and a negative attitude both among supervisors and among the workers.

A co-operative approach to management, the breaking down of entrenched positions, the streamlining of management, the decentralisation of decision making and the need for planning are no doubt all questions that in any case have to be faced in undertakings concerned to apply modern management methods. If, however, the system of flexible working hours prompted such undertakings to give serious attention to these questions, it would indirectly have favourable effects for all concerned.

ADVANTAGES FOR THE WORKERS

The advantages of flexible working hours for the workers can be summed up as greater freedom, the abolition of checks on punctuality, the cessation of gratuitous work, the abolition of privileges, adjustment to the individual's routine and life style, better use of leisure, a fuller social life and a better atmosphere at work.

By its very nature, the system of flexible hours of work has as its first effect that of enhancing the workers' freedom of action in the sense that it enables them within certain limits to arrange their time and hours of work as they please so as to adjust them to their personal needs. At a time when material constraints of all kinds abound, this advantage is, from the psychological point of view, extremely important even for people who, for temperamental reasons, make no use of it. Moreover, this enhanced freedom of action implies an abandonment of the checks on punctuality at the beginning and end of the day's work, because there is no longer any need for them with flexible hours. It is true that under the new system the recording of hours of attendance by a time clock bears a superficial resemblance to earlier checks on punctuality, but in fact the record is only for the purpose of providing evidence of the number of hours worked, so that the question of punctuality no longer arises. Thus the workers no longer have to worry about whether they will arrive in time in the morning and whether, after finishing work, they will be able to arrive in time for an appointment or to be ready in time not to miss the start of a meeting or a show, etc. It follows that there can be a diminution of emotional stresses and of overwork.

Fexible hours entail the cessation of gratuitous work. It is no longer the scheduled hours of work but only the hours of actual attendance that are recorded, so that the minutes which a worker formerly gave freely to the employer by arriving earlier or leaving later are now included in the hours worked and paid for. In other words, work that was done for nothing by the zealous employee becomes work offset by time off, thereby affording greater scope for the organisation of leisure time.

Another advantage is the abolition of privileges. When hours of work are rigidly scheduled it is often accepted that certain categories of personnel, especially office workers and supervisory staff, need not keep strictly to the scheduled hours. The introduction of the system of flexible working hours puts an end to these privileges or advantages attached to positions and rank, whether for whole categories of staff or for individuals.

Under the new system the worker is also better able to adjust his hours of work to his daily routine. For example, the early riser can begin work earlier than the worker who prefers to go to bed late. In fact the system of flexible working hours enables the worker to adjust his hours of work not only to his daily routine but also to his individual way of life. For example, workers who have to travel only a relatively short distance to go to work and who want to go home at midday can choose a long break, while others may prefer a short midday break and to leave early at the end of their day's work. If the husband and wife in a household both work, they can arrange among themselves when to start and finish work so as to suit their children's school hours. In this way it becomes possible to ensure a better adjustment of hours of work to family needs.

However, the main advantage for the workers is no doubt the improvement in the quality of leisure time. The system of flexible working hours enables them to avoid traffic hold-ups on their way to work if they have their own means of transport, and to choose the most convenient service, with the least waiting time, if they use public transport. It also enables them to choose at their convenience the times of the day for shopping and to make the best use of them, thereby reducing "unproductive" free time to a minimum. The amount of leisure time that can be arranged at will is increased, with a resulting improvement in the quality of the individual's leisure as a whole. The new system also facilitates social and cultural life and enables more time to be devoted to recreational, cultural and educational pursuits.

Through the better adjustment of hours of work to individual needs, the abolition of tacitly accepted privileges and a diminution of the pressures of modern life, as well as in many other ways, flexible working hours can also contribute not only to an improvement of the general atmosphere and human relations in the undertaking but also to an ultimate enhancement of pleasure in work. For workers who value them, a pleasant atmosphere at work and harmonious working relationships are powerful stimuli. Moreover, in one way or another the staff always benefit in the long run from the resulting increases in productivity.

ADVANTAGES FOR MANAGEMENT

From the employer's point of view, the advantages of flexible hours of work can be listed as higher productivity, a reduction in staff turnover, less waste of working time, less overtime, quicker starting up of work, a diminution of the number of short absences, the charging to the workers of unavoidable delays in coming to work, a postponement of disbursements for credit hours, and improved management.

When the workers benefit from the advantages which the system of flexible hours of work can give them, they find greater satisfaction in their work and have more reasons for taking an interest in the welfare of the undertaking, with a resulting increase in individual output and therefore in productivity. In other words, there is an interaction between the advantages granted to the workers and those from which the undertaking benefits. The increase in productivity may be due to one or more causes such as a reduction of the amount of time required per unit of output, a diminution of waste, a fall in labour turnover or a drop in absenteeism. In this connection it should not be overlooked, however, that innovation is often an incentive in itself. There is a possibility, therefore, that the improvements resulting from the introduction of a system of flexible working hours may subsequently diminish a little.

A good many of the advantages do not flow solely from the improvement of the atmosphere within the undertaking and from mental attitudes; they are of a structural nature, and are therefore enduring. There can be no doubt that a high degree of staff turnover may be attributable, at any rate in part, to an unduly rigid schedule of hours of work. In such a case a change in the traffic and transport situation can prompt some workers to change jobs if the undertaking declines to take the altered situation into account. Also in the case of workers with families there may be a change of jobs if there is a modification of school hours, or where one of the spouses alters his or her hours of work and the other wants to adapt his or her hours accordingly. It is clear that the system of flexible working hours permits the necessary adjustments and thereby contributes to a stabilisation of the workforce.

Another advantage is that there is less time wasted and less overtime. It is quite feasible for the workers to adjust their hours of work to their workload, such an adjustment being, incidentally, in the employer's interest also. There is consequently a reduction of unproductive stand-by time, as well as a diminution in the amount of overtime. Admittedly such an adjustment is not necessarily an effect of flexible working hours; but the system does provide the workers with opportunities for adjustment of which they may avail themselves if they so wish, their own attitude being therefore decisive in this matter.

Flexible working hours can be also of some advantage to the undertaking in that the workers begin their work in accordance with their individual habits and thereby more quickly reach their full productive capacity. As a result, the daily starting up of work can take less time. This point may be viewed also from another angle: where there is a rigid work schedule, it is often necessary to stop certain operations at the time fixed for the closing of workshops of offices, whereas flexible working hours make it possible to complete those operations on the same day if so desired; this avoids starting up work again, re-examining a file, re-assembling the necessary papers and other losses of time.

The number of short absences is also likely to diminish. It is constantly found in undertakings with a fixed schedule that many workers who would have arrived late for work, especially in the morning, prefer to report sick. With flexible working hours such abuses might cease inasmuch as the day's work no longer has to start at a specified time, so that a diminution of short-time absenteeism becomes possible. It has been noticed in some undertakings that the introduction of the new system has been followed by a sharp drop in the number of short absences due to sickness that is more often feigned than genuine; however, this reduction is no doubt also attributable to the abolition of checks on punctuality, as well as—and much more so—to a general improvement in the atmosphere at the workplace.

Many undertakings have turned a blind eye, and still turn a blind eye, to losses of time due to special circumstances (late train arrivals, traffic hold-ups, etc.) or to failures within tolerable limits to abide by scheduled hours of work, no deduction from wages being made. Yet these irretrievably lost hours of work ultimately build up to a not inconsiderable total. For example, a daily loss of five minutes is equal to about 1 per cent of working time. Under the system of flexible working hours, the risks of losses of time of this kind are borne by the workers, so that the undertaking itself does not suffer.

In addition, as regards credit hours which workers try to accumulate in order to carry them forward from period to period, when the credits thus carried forward exceed the debits the undertaking benefits from work that does not have to be paid for until a later stage.

A final point is that if it is to operate in a normal way, the system of flexible hours of work requires that the undertaking shall be well organised, that there shall be well established methods of delegating authority and that decisions shall have been thoroughly considered at all levels. This means that efficient modern methods of management must be adopted, such methods being in any case clearly to the interest of the undertaking.

ADVANTAGES FOR THE ECONOMY AS A WHOLE

Where flexible hours of work lead to an increase in the productivity of undertakings through the inducements that they offer to the staff, a more efficient organisation of work, the application of more scientific methods of management and so on, it contributes *ipso facto* to an increase in the productivity of the economy as a whole.

By enabling peak traffic hours to be avoided and travel time to be suitably distributed, flexible hours can also bring about a reduction in the infrastructure costs to the community through the diminution of pressure on the system of communications.

Flexible hours of work can also help to reduce the frequency of traffic accidents: where hours of work are rigidly scheduled, the check on arrivals incites workers driving their own motor vehicles to look constantly at their watches, and the effects of this on the nervous system can cause accidents in heavy traffic at peak hours.

Flexible working hours also open up new possibilities in the field of recruitment. Where hours are fixed, married women in particular often refrain from taking a job that would require them to follow a timetable differing from their husbands' or from their children's school timetable. The new system is calculated to overcome such obstacles and thereby to increase the potential national supply of labour.

Lastly, any diminution of staff turnover as a result of flexible working hours can be advantageous to the whole economy inasmuch as excessive turnover can in particular give rise to recruitment costs that are by definition unproductive and to hardly profitable expenditure of time in giving induction training to newcomers—all of which leads to an over-all reduction of productivity.

DRAWBACKS FOR THE WORKERS

In point of fact it is much less for the workers in general than for some categories of them that the system of flexible working hours can be disadvantageous in certain respects, though only mildly so. There are, for example, occupations and services for which it is impossible to introduce the system, so that workers who cannot benefit from it may feel deprived when they see the benefits enjoyed by others. This sense of deprivation can also be felt, however, by those who, under a system of rigidly scheduled hours, benefited from special treatment or were hardly if at all subject to checks on their punctuality and attendance. For that matter, flexible working hours can be regarded as somewhat disadvantageous by workers who, owing to the organisation of the undertaking or the distribution of work, have to come to an understanding with their fellow workers in regard to hours of attendance, since under that system it often happens that the weaker members of a group have to bow to the wishes of the stronger.

Flexible hours of work can also have somewhat unfavourable effects for workers whose brief absences (late arrival in the morning, short breaks to settle urgent personal affairs, leaving before time at the end of the day, etc.) did not give rise to wage deductions or could not be made up for. Such absences were usually winked at in the case of workers paid by the month, it being presumed that they also worked now and then after closing time without claiming remuneration for overtime.

Among the unfavourable psychological reactions to flexible hours of work reference must be made also to the virtually unavoidable reintroduction of time clocks. In recent years there have been many successful efforts to abolish these clocks, because it was often felt that their use constituted discrimination between blue-collar workers, on the one hand, and, on the other, white-collar workers who were not obliged to clock in and clock out, and also because they were used in many cases as checks on punctuality and even to penalise lateness. The elimination of time clocks having been regarded as a clear victory for the workers, it is understandable that their reappearance should meet with some opposition. It should not be overlooked in this connection, however, that, with respect to flexible working hours, these clocks perform an entirely different function in that they serve merely to record the hours actually worked by the individual and thereby to enable a correct account to be drawn up. Inasmuch as the recording of hours of attendance is the counterpart of each worker's freedom of decision and is as a rule compulsory for all workers without distinction, it should not be regarded as other than a simple formality. As soon as the workers grasp this fundamental difference between the old system and the new, opposition to the mechanical recording of hours of attendance vanishes, so that the reappearance of time clocks or similar apparatus should no longer be a source of annoyance.

Workers may also lose by unreasonable rules regarding overtime as, for example, when the time that they work at the request of their supervisors outside the theoretical normal hours of work does not entitle them to any increase in rate of pay if it does not exceed the prescribed number of monthly hours of work, account being taken of the credit hours to be carried forward and of the debit hours carried over from the preceding month. This disadvantage can be avoided, however, by settling the question of overtime in a manner acceptable to all concerned.

DRAWBACKS FOR MANAGEMENT

The recording of attendance required under the system of flexible working hours obviously involves undertakings in some expenditure: they have to meet the non-recurring cost of acquiring and installing the necessary apparatus as well as the running costs relating to attendance cards and their checking and analysis. These costs vary widely, of course, with the particular system of flexible hours of work, the organisation and structure of the undertaking and so forth. [1] It is impossible, therefore, to assess their

---

[1] Steffen Hackh: *Gleitende Arbeitszeit* (Munich, 1971), pp. 112 ff.; E. Jörin: "Die gleitende Arbeitszeit", in *Journal des associations patronales suisses,* op. cit., No. 49, 6 Dec. 1973, pp. 869-871; and R. Jäger: "Gleitzeit-Erfahrungen", in *Der Arbeiter* (Cologne), Nos. 22-23, 1971, p. 1047.

exact amount but, on the basis of the available information, it does not appear that they constitute an insurmountable obstacle to the introduction of flexible working hours.

Since the new system makes it necessary for the undertaking to remain open longer, there are supplementary costs relating in particular to the running of heating, lighting and power installations and to the manning of the entrance to the buildings, the telephone switchboard, etc. As the hours of servicing may exceed the normal hours of work by 25 to 30 per cent, the expense may in certain cases be quite considerable.

For an undertaking that has been strictly checking arrivals but whose staff may fairly often have worked on, generally without pay, for a few minutes beyond the closing time of the workshops or offices, adoption of the system of flexible working hours can have the disadvantage of compelling the management to pay or compensate with time off the minutes worked gratuitously, which in time build up into hours.

Moreover, the flexible working hours system may in the long run compel the employer to give some sort of compensation to workers who, for technical or organisational reasons, are required to work fixed hours. For the time being this risk is no doubt still quite small, but it is to be expected that it will grow as the new system spreads.

Furthermore, it is possible that here and there the flexible working hours system will raise internal difficulties of communication resulting in unused time, bottlenecks and general friction. Where these difficulties cannot be overcome, the smooth working of the undertaking might be jeopardised.

The flexible hours of work system presupposes that the employer has faith in the sense of responsibility and the honesty of his staff. It can happen, of course, that some of them abuse that trust for a fairly long time without being found out. Their untrustworthiness, should it become too grievous, could be of no small financial disadvantage to the undertaking, and even if it is slight it can spoil the atmosphere at work by causing the more scrupulous staff to object to behaviour which they regard as disloyal. It is a good sign when the staff itself calls for checks in order to put a stop to such abuses.

SPECIAL PROBLEMS

4

THE ORGANISATION OF WORK

Although the modern economy rests on the application of the principle of division of labour, no undertaking could allow its various activities to be so separated as to interfere with its smooth working. On the contrary, the greater the degree of division of labour the more do functions and jobs become interdependent, so that continuous co-operation and co-ordination become a necessity. This appears very clearly in such fields as assembly-line work and transport within the undertaking. There is, however, interdependence also in the administrative field whether at the top executive level or in data processing or in internal communications, etc., and some services must be maintained throughout the working hours of the undertaking, especially in the case of watchmen and staff in charge of security, heating, power supply and repairs.

Flexible working hours raise special problems not only because of the interdependence of functions and jobs but also in connection with the undertaking's external economic and social relations. The relations between customers and suppliers depend, in so far as they are of a personal nature, on arrangements made jointly during visits and meetings; but with flexible hours of work only one of the parties is free arrange meetings outside the period of compulsory attendance, so that personal contacts may no longer be feasible. This problem of the influence of flexible working hours on external relations faces all undertakings, but is especially acute for those in the services sector, where personal contacts are necessary.

It should also be noted that in certain activities punctuality is essential. For example, the regularity and punctuality of public transport services, which have to keep to definite timetables, are not to be jeopardised by a system allowing the operating staff to dispose freely of its time. Similarly, theatres, concerts, the mass media and many other institutions depend on compliance with certain rules of punctuality.

It has to be admitted that the system of flexible working hours does not suit all categories of undertakings and all jobs, but it would be pushing uniformity too far to set the system aside solely on that account. Consequently before a decision is taken on the expediency of introducing it there must be a thoroughgoing analysis of the facts and of organisational possibilities with regard to such matters as the interdependence of functions and jobs and the permanent services to be manned. Experience shows that when this is done flexible working hours can be applied much more widely than is commonly supposed.

The system may seem at first sight to be wholly incompatible with assembly-line work [1], especially where it has to be done at a specified pace; but owing to absenteeism, holidays, etc., many undertakings which employ this method of work already have to alleviate the demand that it makes on the operator by providing for various forms of relief such as stand-by operators, overlapping spheres of operations and double occupancy of certain posts. With the prior agreement of those concerned, provision can be made for such relief at the time of introduction of the system of flexible hours of work. Nevertheless the system is unlikely to be generally adopted by undertakings practising rigidly paced assembly-line work.

Things are different where assembly-line work is not subject to a particular rhythm. It is then possible as a rule to hold small "buffer stocks" at intermediate points along the line; each operator is responsible for seeing to it that the next worker down the line shall find enough work to last for the whole period of optional attendance, and no worker may leave until a sufficient stock has been provided to keep the worker next in line occupied until leaving work. This system has already been applied with success, especially in the clock and watch-making and office machinery industries. [2] However, there are limits to the application of the system; in particular it is not profitable where the buffer stocks take up a lot of room, as is shown

---

[1] It is claimed that, by reason of new psychological and sociological theories, assembly-line work will increasingly be superseded by team work. Without pausing here to consider this claim, it will suffice to indicate that, so far as application of the system of flexible hours of work is concerned, fewer problems of organisation arise with team work than with assembly-line work.

[2] In this way the Omega watch factory at Bienne has enabled workers operating the Lenco assembly-line system to benefit from flexible hours of work. For a more detailed description, see B. J. Zumsteg: *L'horaire libre dans l'entreprise, ses causes, ses problèmes, ses conséquences* (Neuchâtel, Delachaux & Niestlé, 1971), pp. 55 ff. For the experiment made by the firm of Assmann at Bad Homburg, see Hackh, op. cit. pp. 118 ff., and L. Sareyka: *Vergleichende Untersuchung über die Erfahrungen nach Einführung der Gleitzeit aus Berichten von mehr als 150 Unternehmen (Industrie, Handel, Verbände und Verwaltung)* (Mönchengladbach, 1971).

in the following passage from an official French report to which reference has already been made [1]:

(a) The system of flexible working hours appears to be compatible with assembly-line work when the items to be assembled are small, so that an intermediate stock can be maintained between two stations.

(b) It should be possible to apply the system also within certain limits to assembly lines manned by a small number of workers (Brown-Boveri) whether because of the nature of the product or because of a division of a long line into several sub-lines, but subject, of course, to agreement among the members of the team and to an increase in the skill of each member.

(c) On the other hand it must be admitted that it is difficult to overcome the obstacles to flexible hours on assembly-line work with heavy and bulky items. Such is the case, in particular, with the present form of the main assembly lines in motor vehicle manufacture owing to the very nature of the work, which calls for a very detailed division of operations and the simultaneous participation of all the operators.

Apart from assembly-line work, interdependent jobs are frequently performed by teams. The members of each team must then agree on the question of arrangement of hours of work. If a team is well broken in, its members are usually ready to co-operate closely and to agree among themselves, so that there need be no difficulty in operating the system of flexible working hours. If difficulties do exist, however, a question that arises is whether, from the angle of group dynamics, the composition of the team is such as to conduce to optimum output, irrespective of flexible hours. However that may be, there are plenty of cases to show that it is quite possible in practice to bring about a spirit of mutual understanding within groups of workers. Thus a specialised foundry which had decided to leave teams of five to eight persons in its casting and assembly departments entirely free to arrange their hours of work expressed itself as follows in a report on its experience: "The members of each team have always got on so well together with regard to their respective hours of work that there has never been any disturbance of the production process."

In the case of services that have to be maintained on a permanent footing, the introduction of the system of flexible hours of work also raises difficulties, though not all of them are insurmountable. Experience has shown that some of those services depend on the number of persons actually at work. By definition the members of the staff are not all present in the undertaking during the period of optional attendance. Consequently some services, such as the telephone switchboard, distribution of supplies, etc., are less heavily worked during that period than during the period of compulsory attendance. As a result, the staffing of those services can be dimin-

---

[1] de Chalendar, op. cit., p. 24.

ished either by making application of the system of flexible working hours conditional on a requirement that those concerned shall agree among themselves with regard to the maintenance of the necessary skeleton staff or by issuing instructions that they should take turns to be on duty during the period of optional attendance. By way of illustration, this is what a large undertaking had to say about its telephone switchboard employing 14 persons: "Since there is less telephoning during the period of optional attendance, one or two telephone operators suffice. That is why we have decided that, taking it in turns, only one operator need be on duty in the morning and only two at the end of the day, the remainder working flexible hours."

In undertakings applying flexible hours of work it is sometimes difficult to reach certain persons outside the period of compulsory attendance. Customers and suppliers often hesitate on that account to telephone or to call in without warning at certain times in order to contact particular members of the staff since there is no certainty that they will be in their offices. For that matter, is there any certainty even where an undertaking works to a rigid schedule? Nowadays, with the ever growing number of meetings and interviews both within and outside the undertaking, the executive staff are not constantly available, so that flexible hours of work could not lead to any fundamental changes. On the other hand, they might call for a general improvement of the flow of information and an extension of the practice of appointing substitutes so that contacts can be ensured. For that matter, such measures might be applied throughout the working day, including the period of compulsory attendance.

Thus the drawbacks of flexible hours of work for undertakings having frequent and close relations with the outside world lie less in the difficulty of contacting certain persons than in the possibility of ensuring that they will be available at particular times. In the services sector, for example, banks, transport undertakings and the offices of public authorities, to mention only these cases, have to be open at definite hours. As for large stores, retail shops, travel agencies, etc., they are generally open during periods coinciding with the hours of work of employees. On the other hand, it is obviously out of the question to make all these hours of opening coincide exactly with the usual period of compulsory attendance, because the flow of customers and visitors is likely to be at its peak just when the staff of other undertakings takes advantage of the choice of hours which the flexible working hours system makes available to them. Yet some establishments in the services sector have not balked at these difficulties. In Switzerland, in particular, various banks have introduced flexible hours of work, having considered that, since only some of the staff were needed to deal with customers, it was quite feasible to provide the service required by requesting selected employees to arrange among themselves the organisation of the necessary rotation, provided, of course, that the selected employees were capable of handling a variety of tasks. [1] Certain government departments and similar institutions have also adopted solutions of that kind.

Nevertheless, one should not close one's eyes to the fact that the system of flexible working hours is unlikely to find much support among undertakings in the services sector that have to remain constantly at the disposal of their customers, as is the case especially with hotels and retail shops. This point applies also to services that have to be provided at regular intervals (public transport).

SHIFT WORK

As a rule shift work may be necessary for two different reasons—

(a) in order to enable production equipment that has required a heavy investment of capital to be used for a longer stretch of time; and

(b) in order to carry out successfully processes that do not lend themselves to any interruption and that take longer than the working day to complete.

Where there has to be recourse to shift work because an interruption of the production process is not technically feasible, there has to be a continuous succession of shifts, so that there is little scope for flexible working hours; on the other hand, where recourse is had to shift work solely for the purpose of using costly equipment for a longer stretch of time, that is primarily for economic reasons, an uninterrupted succession of shifts is no longer essential.

The flexible working hours system presupposes that the working hours of the undertaking are appreciably longer than the prescribed hours of work. If flexible hours are introduced also for shift work, that margin must be retained so that the optional working hours of two differents shifts will not overlap unduly; otherwise some positions might be temporarily occupied uneconomically by two persons.

All these considerations lead up to the conclusion that with a three-shift system the time available for any one shift is not sufficient to enable it to work optional hours outside the scheduled hours of work. As the time-table of a Swiss engineering firm shows, if the scheduled hours of work

---

[1] See in this connection de Chalendar, op. cit., p. 26.

Table 5.   Timetable for a three-shift system

Shift	Work period	Break
First shift	5.45 a.m. to 2 p.m.	8.50 to 9.20 a.m.
Second shift	1.45 p.m. to 10 p.m.	6 to 6.30 p.m.
Third shift	9.45 p.m. to 6 a.m.	2 to 2.30 a.m.

amount to 8¼ per day (including a 30-minute break), there is already an overlap of a quarter of an hour (table 5).

This shows that flexible working hours could not be adapted to a three-shift system where the prescribed number of hours of work per day is eight. The only possible solution would be to modify slightly the opening and closing times of the shifts with the agreement of those concerned and in accordance with the practice of many undertakings in exceptional cases, as appears from the following quotation:

The times laid down for changes of shift are fixed. In the timekeeping, deviations of ± five minutes are tolerated. In agreement with the supervisor and the members of the shift, the change-over time may be delayed on certain days in exceptional cases by not more than 30 minutes.

Thus flexible working hours in the proper sense of the term are incompatible with three-shift working, although some arrangements of an exceptional nature, such as those that have just been mentioned, enable some adjustment of the system to be made.

The two-shift system does offer wider possibilities, even if the two shifts have to follow one another without a break. Thus, as the timetable followed in the above-mentioned Swiss engineering firm shows, provision can be made for an optional margin of time at the beginning of the first shift and at the end of the second (table 6).

That the optional margin is, in this case, relatively short, namely of only one hour, is largely due to the fact that owing to the need to avoid any interruption in the succession of shifts provision for such a margin can be made only at the beginning or end of a shift's timetable. In order to comply with the prescribed duration of work, rather less than one-half of the margin can be used on the average. This means that it is not possible to accumulate substantial credits or debits of hours in the course of an accounting period.

This example shows that the system of flexible working hours is not necessarily inapplicable to two-shift work, provided that no technical obstacles relating to production stand in its way. It also shows, however, that the choices open to the worker are limited, so that the advantages of

Table 6. Timetable of a two-shift system with flexible working hours

	Monday-Friday						
First	4.51	5.35	5.51	8.50	9.20		2
(morning)	:......:......:		:	——————	————————————		× p.m.
shift	4.85	5.60	5.85	8.83	9.33		2
	Saturday						
	4.51	5.21	5.51	8.50	9.05	10.36	11.06	11.36
	:......:......:	————————	———————	:	:......:.........:			
	4.85	5.35	5.85	8.83	9.08	10.60	11.10	11.60
	Monday-Friday						
Second	2		6	6.30		10.30	11.09	11.30
(afternoon)	×	——————	——————	:	:......:.........:			
shift	2		6	6.50		10.50	11.15	11.50

————— Core time .... Optional period × Change of shift ———— Break (fixed, no timekeeping) : Beginning or end of work (average).

In the two-shift system and taking into account the timetables of the shifts, the opening time of the first shift and the closing time of the second shift may be chosen freely within the limits of the optional period, provided that other restrictions are not needed for operational reasons.

No overlapping of the timetables of the shift workers is allowed. The time for the change of shift in accordance with the timetables of the two shifts is fixed. A time-keeping error of ± five minutes is tolerated. On certain days and in exceptional circumstances, the end of the first shift's work may be advanced by a maximum of 30 minutes and the beginning of the second shift's work may be retarded by a maximum of 30 minutes, subject to the agreement of the supervisor.

flexible working hours are rather slender. In fact that is why the system is only infrequently applied to shift workers.

TIME RECORDING

One of the most difficult problems connected with flexible working hours concerns the recording of attendance, because it brings into play a variety of organisational, technical, psychological and other factors. The times of attendance are recorded by means of special cards. In general, these cards have to be stamped by a time clock at the beginning and end of the day and for each break. In a few cases the system of mechanical recording has been abandoned: the worker himself makes the necessary entries by hand. It is to be noted, however, that this method, which makes it possible to dispense with time clocks, has itself been abandoned in a few undertakings at the express request of the staff with a view to prevention, where technically feasible, of any slackness.

For legal reasons, the use of time meters is as a rule precluded because they merely add up the hours worked without proving, as is required by

(text continued on p. 52)

Figure 2. Simple attendance card

Department _____   Name _____

Pay from _____ to _____   19 _____

Date	Morning		Afternoon		Break		Attendance time		
	Arrival	Departure	Arrival	Departure	Departure	Return	Total number of hours	Normal hours	Overtime

Figure 3. Time sheet

Month _____ Department _____ Name _____

Standard working day (in minutes) _____

Day	Attendance as recorded on card		Carry-over from preceding month	Absences to be deducted	Reason	Total time worked	Credit time	Debit time	Balance ±
	Normal hours	Overtime				Min.	Min.	Min.	Min.
1st									
2nd									
3rd									
31st									

law, that there has been compliance with the maximum daily and weekly numbers of hours of work and with breaks. In any case, with meters it is necessary to use other means of recording absences, overtime, etc.

The most widely used system, which is based on mutual trust, consists in recording mechanically with a time clock the times of arrival and departure and, where necessary, recording by hand absences and their causes, etc. These recordings are usually made by means of numbers or letters forming part of a code, thereby enabling the larger undertakings to process them on their computers with an automatic card reader. In this way it is possible to provide retrospective evidence as is often required by law; to establish jointly hours of attendance and absences with the reasons therefor; and to process the various data automatically. Each worker can check at any time the accuracy of the data recorded. With the system of flexible working hours it is necessary that members of the staff should be able to compare at any time the hours which they have actually worked with the prescribed hours of work so as to determine whether they have already accumulated a credit or a debit during the period of optional attendance. Such comparison can be facilitated by means of indications of the prescribed hours of work for the accounting period, the average prescribed daily number of hours of work, the carry-over from the previous accounting period of the balance of hours relating to the period of optional attendance, etc.; but the workers will generally have to calculate the number of hours which they have actually worked by adding up—with some difficulty at times—the hours stamped by the time clock, and to calculate the deviations from the hours shown.

There is a wide variety of systems of mechanical recording of hours of attendance. It will suffice here to give only two examples of them.

In a small wholesale cosmetics undertaking, the following method has been chosen: all the workers must make use of an attendance card (see figure 2) for recording by means of a time clock their arrivals and departures in the morning and in the afternoon, as well as any absences. When recording by means of a time clock is not feasible, it is done by hand. The workers themselves calculate and record by hand their total hours of attendance, distinguishing between normal hours and overtime. For the other required particulars, use is made of a time sheet which each employee has to fill by hand and on which there are various headings, as figure 3 shows. The last column makes it possible for those who so wish to record at any time their balance of credits or debits. Experience has shown that in the undertaking in question workers needed from 30 to 50 seconds a day to stamp their cards and to fill in their time sheet.

In relatively large undertakings attendances are generally recorded by means of special apparatus so that the cards can be read by data-processing equipment. This calls for detailed instructions relating to the various operations. As a rule, however, it is found that if the workers have been carefully instructed they quickly master these operations, which may seem complicated at first sight. In this connection, the text reproduced below, which comes from a fairly large Swiss electricity undertaking, is of interest. (A specimen of the attendance card itself is given on the next page.)

Instructions for individual time recording

1. Recording apparatus

Attendance is recorded in hours and hundredths of an hour by means of the special apparatus installed in each department.

2. Attendance card

Use will be made of attendance card, format 3,256.7 white,
— for a whole calendar week from Monday to Sunday, *or*
— for part of a week at the end or beginning of a month.
The card must be placed in the pigeon-holes provided for all workers in the department, as follows:
— in the "present" pigeon-hole during working time;
— in the "absent" pigeon-hole in the event of absence.
The card is taken out of the pigeon-hole only in the following cases:
— for making an entry;
— for any checks;
— at the end of the week or month.

The card must never be kept in one's pocket!

At the end of the week
— normally on Friday evening,
— exceptionally on Saturday or Sunday, *or*
— at the end of the month (last day of work),
the card must be placed in the wooden container located next to the pigeon-holes.

3. Recording of hours of work

The hours of work are recorded on the card—
(a) *mechanically,* by means of the apparatus situated in each department, *by the workers concerned themselves,*
— at the beginning and end of their work;
— at the beginning and end of their midday break;
— on the occasion of other interruptions of work;
(b) *by hand,* entering the day and the time in hours and minutes (making a total of five digits as shown on the speciment card),

(text continued on p. 56)

Front of card

Identification

a) Identification code *or*

b) Handwritten entries of first name, surname, telephone or department and register numbers, year, month and week

Handwritten entries

a) On left-hand side of card:

Holidays in days and half-days;

Military service in days and half-days;

Absences to be entered in two rows
   Upper row: reason for absence (code number, as shown in code on back of card);
   Lower row: *beginning* of absence as stamped or entered by hand *or* 00 for all absences since the beginning of the day.

b) On right-hand side of card:

Entries of times (overlooked timekeepings, absences away from the locality, duty travel):

Day of week (Nos. 1–7); hours and minutes.

Entries here *not* to be made by hand.

This space is *solely* for time recording with the special apparatus.

Invalid time recordings must not be crossed out but cancelled with code No. 80 and the number of the appropriate row.

The times are recorded in hours and hundredths of an hour.

Handwritten entries by the Control Service: Total of days and weeks.

Handwritten entries:

Overtime A (6 a.m. to 8 p.m.)
Overtime B (nights and Sundays)
in hours and tenths of an hour.

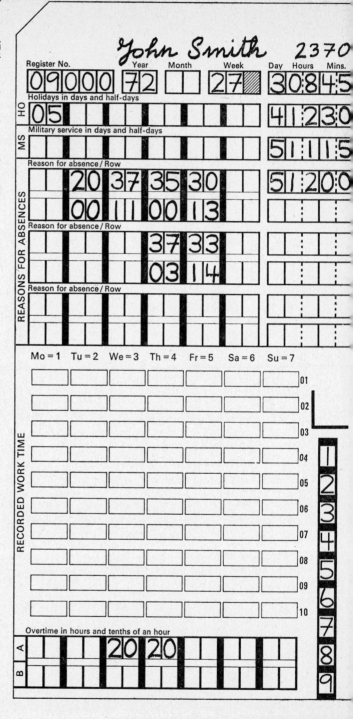

54

Supervisor's endorsement						
Mo	Tu	We	Th	Fr	Sa	Su/wk

Absence coding list

Blood donors scheme	36	Non-industrial accident	41
Compensation for overtime	76	Public duty in accordance with section 18 of rules relating to absences	30
Confinement	23		
Dentist—see visit to doctor		Reduction of hours of work (percentage) on account of:	
Designation to visit sick person or to attend funeral of staff member	38	— sickness and treatment — industrial accident and treatment — non-industrial accident and treatment	24 43 44
Duty travel	37	Sickness and treatment	20
Family event relating to a close relation (as defined in the rules)	34	Summons issued by a public authority	77
Family event relating to more distant relations, or acquaintances	59	Training:	
Fire service:		— apprentices in accordance with Personnel Service instructions	35
— active service and fire drill in the undertaking — community fire drill	33 55	— other training and educational activities	46
House removal	32	Visit to doctor or dentist:	
Housekeeping leave of absence expressly requested (only when not taken into account through a reduction of hours of work)	64	— sickness — industrial accident — non-industrial accident — examination for admission to employment	21 40 41 36
Industrial accident	40	Other absences not mentioned above:	
Invalid time recording	80		
Military service or civil defence (odd hours only)	22	— expressly applied for — not applied for	65 77

IN CASE OF DOUBT REFER TO THE RULES

Handwritten entries

1. Entries of times (right-hand side of card, upper part).
   Illustration: Time recording overlooked for Thursday, 4.58 p.m.

Day   Hour   Min.

2. Entries of absences (correction):

Illustration: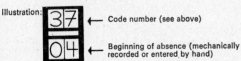

← Code number (see above)

← Beginning of absence (mechanically recorded or entered by hand)

HOURS WORKED MUST BE RECORDED BY THE WORKER IN PERSON

Entries by hand

 Correct

Incorrect

Write each figure *large* enough to fill the space.

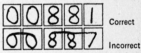 Correct

Incorrect

The loops in 0, 6, 8 and 9 *must be closed.* The loops in 6 and 9 should take up 30–50% of the total height of the figure.

 Correct

Incorrect

Write plainly, without flourishes.

Correct

Incorrect

Don't join the figures together.

Correct

Incorrect

Figures 4 and 5 must be written in unbroken lines.

For all handwritten entries always use a lead pencil, preferably No. 2 or HB (no ball-point, drawing pencil, ordinary ink or Indian ink); write figures as shown above.

55

— in the case of duties outside the factory;
— when mechanical recording has been inadvertently omitted;
— in cases of breakdown of the apparatus.

Absences

Holidays and military service

To be entered by hand in the appropriate day's box or row, as follows: 1.0 = 1 whole day *or* 0.5 = half a day.

Other absences

To be entered by hand in the appropriate day's box:
— the appropriate reference number as shown in the code on the attendance card;
— the beginning of the absence (as stamped or entered by hand)

or

— 00 in cases of whole-day absences, half-day absences in the morning and absences at the beginning of the day.

Overtime

Overtime actually worked must be recorded by hand in hours and tenths of an hour (0.1 = 6 minutes) in row—
— A, for overtime between 6 a.m. and 8 p.m.;
— B, for night and Sunday overtime.

The requirements regarding endorsement of the various handwritten entries are laid down separately for each case.

The recording of attendance raises problems that are not only organisational and technical but also psychological. Most of the methods that are in fact employed involve the use of mechanical apparatus such as time clocks or meters. Such apparatus was already in use in undertakings working fixed hours. It was used to check the punctuality of the staff, and was regarded by them as a symbol of servitude. In recent years trade unions have gradually been able to induce employers to abandon time clocks, and the question therefore arises whether it is expedient to make use once again, for the purposes of flexible working hours, of mechanical apparatus for the recording of attendance. It is after all understandable that the re-establishment of the former checks should meet here and there with objections if not with definite opposition. It should not be overlooked, however, that there is a basic difference between the old system of clocking-in and clocking-out and the mechanical recording of attendance as practised for flexible working hours purposes. Whereas the time clock was an instrument of control and often also of discrimination since it affected as a rule only the workers, office staff being exempt, the mechanical recording of attendance is no more than the corollary of the independence enjoyed by each worker, who can thereby obtain the data needed to claim payment for the hours actually worked.

The experience of various undertakings shows that it is possible by careful presentation to make workers understand this fundamental difference and to rid them of their prejudices against the mechanical recording of attendance. This holds true not only for blue-collar workers but also for office staff. [1]

PREPARATIONS FOR THE INTRODUCTION OF THE SYSTEM

Three prerequisites must be fulfilled if the hopes placed in the system of flexible working hours are to be realised. In the first place the system must be adapted to the needs of the undertaking and the staff. Its introduction must be preceded, therefore, by detailed investigations, especially in the fields of management, organisation and production. It is necessary also to consider carefully the legal implications, the transport situation, problems of communication and the preferences of those concerned so that the system introduced will suit both the undertaking and the staff and will at the same time be acceptable both from the statutory point of view and from the angle of the provisions of the particular collective agreements that are applicable. However, even the best of systems could not survive the unavoidable initial difficulties if the staff were not given full information on its nature, on the problems that it raises and on its practical application. That is the second prerequisite. It is indeed obvious that no innovation is likely to be accepted unless all those concerned have had an opportunity of expressing a view in the light of a full knowledge of the facts. Being aware of that need, most of the undertakings, whether large or small, wishing to introduce flexible hours of work have been careful to prepare the way by issuing information bulletins, rules and instructions illustrated with simple examples. For practical as well as psychological reasons, a good many undertakings at first applied the system only in some departments and experimentally for a certain time. On the basis of the experience acquired and when the reactions of the staff were favourable, they subsequently decided to make the whole of their staff benefit from the system. A large Swiss engineering firm proceeded as follows:

On 1st March 1970, ... the firm ... began to introduce flexible working time. A first experiment was carried out in three departments employing 700

---

[1] R. Schultz: "Grundfragen der gleitenden Arbeitszeit", in *Der Betrieb* (Düsseldorf), No. 6, 1971, p. 251; H. Knebel: "Überlegungen zur Einführung einer wirtschaftlich vertretbaren gleitenden Arbeitszeit", in *Arbeit und Leistung* (Frechen-Köln), No. 12, 1970, p. 218; and Union centrale des Associations patronales suisses: "Expérience avec l'horaire mobile de travail", op. cit.

workers. The results were conclusive and the experiment was extended in the same year to some 2,000 employees; it was also decided to introduce flexible working time gradually . . . wherever this could be done without adversely affecting operations. Today 8,000 employees have the benefit of flexible working time. . . . [1]

Thirdly, the introduction of flexible working hours requires close co-operation between the management of the undertaking, the staff, their representatives and the trade unions. Consulting the staff and their representatives at the preparatory and planning stages has proved very useful, and indeed in most cases essential.

It was realised almost everywhere that careful preparations were necessary. It will suffice in this connection to quote the following passage from the report of an undertaking:

First of all, the general principles of the system and its methods were defined with the co-operation of certain representatives of the staff. The system selected, the provisional arrangements and the plan of implementation were then submitted to the representatives of the staff, who approved them. All the members of the staff were then duly informed. The plan provided for an experimental introduction of the system in four departments, two of them in the management sector and the two others in the production sector; the system was then to be extended to the whole of the management sector after a year's trial and to the whole of the production sector at the end of two years. The trials gave positive results which did not fail to come to the knowledge of the other workers. The representatives of the staff accordingly requested that the date laid down in the plan of application should be brought forward, a request to which it was possible to give effect in the management sector. On the other hand, the complexity of problems in the production sector made it necessary to carry out further investigations so that it was not possible to bring forward the date that had been laid down. Prior to the introduction of flexible hours of work, all the members of the staff were provided with the necessary documentary material, including the text of the provisional arrangements. They were then well informed by means of a sound film, as well as by word of mouth at meetings of about one hour for each group. [2]

---

[1] H. Allenspach : "Working hours per week and day: Flexible working time", in Organisation for Economic Co-operation and Development, Manpower and Social Affairs Directorate: *New patterns for working time,* supplement to the final report, international conference, Paris, 1972, International Seminars 1972—1, pp. 90-91.

[2] E. Jörin, op. cit.

CONCLUSION

5

The reports of the experience of undertakings having adopted the system of flexible working hours provide evidence that the workers employed under it would not want to return to the old system of a rigidly scheduled distribution of hours of work; this evidence is amply corroborated by the results of inquiries made and polls taken in many places after the introduction of the new system whether on a provisional or a permanent basis. This is in any case hardly surprising inasmuch as flexible working hours suit both the workers wishing to take advantage of the flexibility and those who prefer to go on beginning and ending their day's work at regular hours: the system enables everyone to schedule their hours of work in a different way every day, without obliging anyone to do so. Most workers generally deviate from their previous timetable by only a small margin (plus or minus 15 to 30 minutes), and after a while they settle into a new routine.

The system of flexible working hours has hitherto been adopted particularly in Switzerland and in the Federal Republic of Germany; in the other industrialised countries its introduction on a large scale is being carefully considered and a start has already been made. The speed with which the new system has spread is indeed quite surprising: in view of the complexity of the problems to be considered, the practical questions that arise, the information difficulties, the onerous task of suitably amending certain statutory requirements and certain provisions of collective agreements, not to mention the resistance which anything new usually creates, it has to be recognised that in the field of social policy it would hardly be possible to find another innovation that has so quickly and so effectively secured the attention of the parties concerned. Clearly, the greater the experience of the system the more firmly it will establish itself.

Nevertheless, it is also clear that the system could not suit every undertaking and occupation, although the number of workers to whom, for technical or organisational reasons, it does not seem to be applicable is no doubt smaller than is usually supposed. However, the fact that not everybody can have flexible hours is no reason for ruling out the system altogether; after all, night work, Sunday work, shift work, etc., are necessary for certain operations, but there is no question that all workers should be involved in such work. In other words, the system of flexible hours is not the only proper way of distributing work time, any more than any other known system; but on the other hand there are many cases in which it can constitute the best means of meeting a wide variety of requirements and objectives.

BIBLIOGRAPHY

BOOKS

Allenspach, H. "Working hours per week and day: Flexible working time." Organisation for Economic Co-operation and Development, Manpower and Social Affairs Directorate. *New patterns for working time.* Supplement to the final report, international conference, Paris, ... 1972. International Seminars, 1972—1.

Baudraz, J.-F. *L'horaire variable de travail.* Paris, Les Editions d'organisation, 1973.

Baum, St. J., and Young, W. McEwan. *A practical guide to flexible working hours.* London, Kogan Page, 1973.

Bolton, J. H. *Flexible working hours.* Wembley, Middlesex, Anbar Publications, 1971.

Chalendar, J. de. *L'aménagement du temps.* Paris, Desclée de Brouwer, 1971.

— *L'aménagement du temps de travail au niveau de la journée. L'horaire variable ou libre. Rapport du groupe d'études réuni à la demande du Premier ministre.* Paris, La Documentation française, 1972.

Egger, L. *Avantages et inconvénients de l'introduction de la journée de travail à horaire continu, sondage de l'opinion publique.* Lausanne, 1964.

Hackh, St. *Gleitende Arbeitszeit.* Munich, 1971.

Hill, J. M. *Flexible working hours.* London, Institute of Personnel Management, 1973.

International Labour Office. *Human values in social policy: An ILO agenda for Europe,* Report of the Director-General . . . to the Second European Regional Conference, Geneva, ... 1974.

Jeune Chambre économique de Paris. *L'étalement des horaires,* Etude réalisée et diffusée avec le concours du CNAP et de l'Association française pour l'accroissement de la productivité. 1966.

Kapp, B., and Proust, O. *Les horaires libres.* Paris, Chotard, 1973.

Kaemmerer, Christel. *Variable Arbeitszeit — Utopie oder Chance ?* Veröffentlichung der Technischen Akademie e.V. Esslingen. 1970.

— "Personalführung. Motivation und Stimulans menschlicher Arbeitsergiebigkeit". *Variable Arbeitszeit und Gleitzeit.* Wiesbaden, 1971.

Keppler, B. *Die gleitende Arbeitszeit.* Abschlussarbeit an der HWF Pforzheim. 1969.

Knevels, P., and Zehle, R. *Variable Arbeitszeit.* Bergisch Gladbach, 1971.

Mook, W. *Gleitende Arbeitszeit?* Schriftenreihe der Arbeiterkammer Bremen. Bremen, 1970.

Sareyka, L. *Vergleichende Untersuchung über die Erfahrungen nach Einführung der Gleitzeit aus Berichten von mehr als 150 Unternehmen (Industrie, Handel, Verbände und Verwaltung).* Mönchengladbach, 1971.

Schupeta, E. *Gleitende Arbeitszeit.* Taschenbuch für kaufmännische Angestellte in Industrie und Handel. 1971.

Schüt, F. W. *Gleitende Arbeitszeit.* 1971.

Tega, V. *Les horaires flexibles et la semaine réduite de travail.* Montreal, Ecole des hautes études commerciales, 1973.

Le Vert, P. *L'étalement des activités—travail, transport, loisirs.* Paris, Fayard-Mame, 1972.

Zumsteg, B. J. *L'horaire libre dans l'entreprise — ses causes, ses problèmes, ses conséquences.* Neuchâtel, Delachaux & Niestlé, 1971.

PERIODICALS

Allenspach, H. "Flexible working time". *Occupational Psychology* (London, National Institute of Industrial Psychology), 1972, p. 46.

Amman, R. "Les horaires flexibles". *Personnel* (Paris), No. 142 (May 1971).

Barraux, J. "Horaires de travail : à la carte ? ". *Entreprise* (Paris), No. 837 (1971).

Beaujean, C. "Avantages et inconvénients de l'horaire de travail à la carte". *Le Creuset* (Paris, Confédération générale des cadres), 1971.

Belan, H. and Amman, R. "Horaire flexible, durée du travail, législation du travail, absentéisme... ". *Personnel* (Paris), No. 142 (May 1971).

Bishop, T. "Give and take in the working day". *Personnel Management* (London), Vol. 4, No. 6.

Comité pour l'étude et l'aménagement des temps de travail et des temps de loisirs dans la région parisienne (CATRAL). "Horaire variable". *Liaisons sociales* (Paris, Bref social), 1972, No. 2.

Dreetz, K. H. "Grundsätze der gleitenden Arbeitszeit". *Wirtschaft und Wissen* (Cologne), 1970, No. 3.

— "Des heures de travail à la carte". *Monde du travail libre* (Brussels, International Confederation of Free Trade Unions), June 1970.

Droog, J. de. "Conditions préalables à la bonne marche de l'horaire variable. Répercussions fonctionnelles sur l'entreprise et psychologiques sur le personnel". *L'entreprise et l'homme* (Brussels, Association des dirigeants et cadres chrétiens), No. 1, 1973.

Eckert, H. "Die Gleitzeit, Motive — Erfahrungen — Perspektiven". *Deutsches Industrienstitut — Beiträge zur Sozialpolitik,* 1971, No. 7.

Haller W. "Die Neuordnung der Zeit". *Arbeit und Leistung* (Frechen/Cologne), 1972, No. 6.

Hammond, B. "A time for Gleitzeit". *Business administration* (London), January 1972.

— "Gliding time comes to Britain". *New Scientist and Science Journal* (London), Vol. 53, No. 787, March 1972.

Henner, D. "L'horaire dynamique — Une enquête". *Analyse et prévision* (Paris, Sedeis), 14 December 1972.

Hildebrandt, W. and Littow, E. "Erfahrungen mit der variablen Arbeitszeit in Unternehmen und Behörden — Ergebnisse einer Umfrage". *Arbeit und Leistung* (Frechen/Cologne), 1971, No. 6.

Hillert, A. "Gleitende Arbeitszeit — Beispiel moderner Arbeitsorganisation". *Die Aussprache* (Bonn/Bad Godesberg), 1969, No. 10.

— "Praktische Erfahrungen mit der Glaz zu Beginn und Ende des Arbeitstages". *Personal, Mensch und Arbeit im Betrieb* (Munich), No. 8, 1968.

— "Rechtsfragen der gleitenden Arbeitszeit". *Der Betriebsberater* (Heidelberg), No. 5/20, (February 1970).

— "Gleitzeit : Profit ? Sozialer Fortschritt ?". *Der Arbeitgeber* (Cologne), 1970, No. 21.

— "Gleitzeit: In gegenseitigen Vertrauen". *Der Arbeitgeber* (Cologne), 1970, No. 22.

— "Arbeitszeit. Zur kontinuierlichen Einarbeitung". *Der Arbeitgeber* (Cologne), 1971, No. 23.

— "Gleitende Arbeitszeit als Instrument der Personalführung". *Personalführung* (Düsseldorf), 1972, No. 10.

Ivaldy, J. P. "L'horaire mobile". *Humanisme et entreprise* (Neuilly, Centre d'études et de recherches), No. 77 (February 1973).

Jäger, R. "Gleitzeit-Erfahrungen". *Der Arbeitgeber* (Cologne), 1971, Nos. 22-23.

Jörin, E. "Die gleitende Arbeitszeit". *Schweizerische Arbeitgeber-Zeitung* (Zurich), 1973, No. 49.

Josten, F. A. "Die gleitende Arbeitszeit als Instrument der Personalpolitik und -führung". *Arbeit und Leistung* (Frechen/Cologne), 1973, No. 12.

Kammerer, Ch. "Wie die variable Arbeitszeit zur Verbesserung des Betriebsklimas führt". *Wirtschaftspraxis,* No. 268 (September 1970).

Knebel, H. "Überlegungen zur Einführung einer wirtschaftlich vertretbaren 'gleitenden' Arbeitszeit". *Arbeit und Leistung* (Frechen/Cologne), 1970, No. 12.

Knevels, P. "Variable Arbeitszeit — pro und contra". *Der Arbeitgeber* (Cologne), 1970, No. 14.

Langholz, B. "Die Kontrolle der gleitenden Arbeitszeit". *Der Betrieb* (Düsseldorf), 1972, No. 12.

Mass, K. "Gleitzeitmodelle". *Gewerkschaftliche Praxis* (Cologne), 1970, No. 5.

Moeller, G. "Gleitende Arbeitszeit". *Die Aussprache* (Bonn/Bad Godesberg), 1970, Nos. 5-6.

Nef, U .Ch ."Rechtiche Aspekte der 'gleitenden Arbeitszeit' ". *Zeitschrift für schweizerisches Recht* (Basle), 1971, No. 90.

Sadler, G. "Zur Problematik der 'gleitenden Arbeitszeit' ". *Zeitschrift für Organisation* (Wiesbaden), July 1970.

Sartin, P. "Les horaires libres". *Travail et méthodes* (Paris), No. 286 (February 1973).

Schmidt, E. "Die gleitende Arbeitszeit und ihre rechtlichen Probleme". *Der Betrieb* (Düsseldorf), 1971, No. 1.

Schonberger, R. J. "Inflexible working conditions keep women 'unliberated' " *Personnel Journal* (Swarthmore), Vol. 50, No. 11.

Schott, R. "Arbeitswissenschaftliche Forderung an eine variable Arbeitszeit". *Fortschrittliche Betriebsführung* (Darmstadt), 1970, No. 4.

— "Arbeitswissenschaftliche Fragen an eine variable Arbeitszeit". *Arbeit und Leistung* (Frechen/Cologne), 1972, No. 6.

Schuberth, Ch. "Voraussetzungen und Folgen einer variablen Arbeitszeit". *Junge Wirtschaft* (Bad Godesberg), 1969, No. 8.

Schulte, B. "Die Arbeitszeit im Blickfeld menschlicher Lebensbedürfnisse". *Arbeit und Leistung* (Frechen/Cologne), 1972, No. 6.

Schultz, R. "Grundfragen der gleitenden Arbeitszeit". *Der Betrieb* (Düsseldorf), 1971, No. 6.

Schupeta, E. "Gleitende Arbeitszeiten — wirtschaftlicher und sozialer Forschritt". *Sozialer Forschritt* (Bonn), 1971, No 3.

— "Sozialpolitische Aspekte der gleitenden Arbeitszeit". *Arbeit und Leistung* (Frechen/Cologne), 1972, No. 6.

Tejmar, J. "Arbeitszeit als rechtlicher, Belastungszeit als physiologischer Begriff: Gegensätze und Kompromisse". *Arbeit und Leistung* (Frechen/Cologne), 1972, No. 6.

Le Vert, P. "L'aménagement des temps de travail". *Ingénieurs et cadres de France* (Paris), No. 128 (May-June 1970).

Waldmann, F. "Die Einführung und Durchführung der flexiblen Arbeitszeit". *Personal, Mensch und Arbeit im Betrieb* (Munich), 1970, No. 4.

Willems, R. and Zimmermann, H. J. "Systeme für die Erfassung der Gleitzeit". *Bürotechnik, Automation und Organisation* (Baden-Baden, Goeller-Verlag), 1970, No. 5.

Wörl, R. "Ein Stückchen Selbstbestimmung". *Der Gewerkschafter* (Winterthur, IG Metall), 1970, No. 7.

Würthner, A. "Stempeln mit Toleranz". *Der Gewerkschafter* (Winterthur), 1970 No. 4.

"Expériences avec l'horaire mobile de travail". *Journal des associations patronales suisses* (Zurich), February-March 1971.

"Flex-time introduced into the manufacturing industry. The promotion of flexible working hours". *Japan Labour Bulletin* (Tokyo, Japan Institute of Labour), Vol. 12, No. 8 (August 1973).

"Horaire variable — Premières expériences et perspectives". *Documents ILEC,* No. 593 (29 March 1972).

"Les expériences d'horaires dynamiques réalisées par les adhérents d'Entreprise et progrès". *Entreprise et progrès,* April 1973.